FIRST 50 POP SONGS

YOU SHOULD PLAY ON BASS

ISBN 978-1-7051-4027-7

Visit Hal Leonard Online at
www.halleonard.com

Contact us:
Hal Leonard
7777 West Bluemound Road
Milwaukee, WI 53213
Email: info@halleonard.com

In Europe, contact:
Hal Leonard Europe Limited
42 Wigmore Street
Marylebone, London, W1U 2RN
Email: info@halleonardeurope.com

In Australia, contact:
Hal Leonard Australia Pty. Ltd.
4 Lentara Court
Cheltenham, Victoria, 3192 Australia
Email: info@halleonard.com.au

All About That Bass

Words and Music by Meghan Trainor and Kevin Kadish

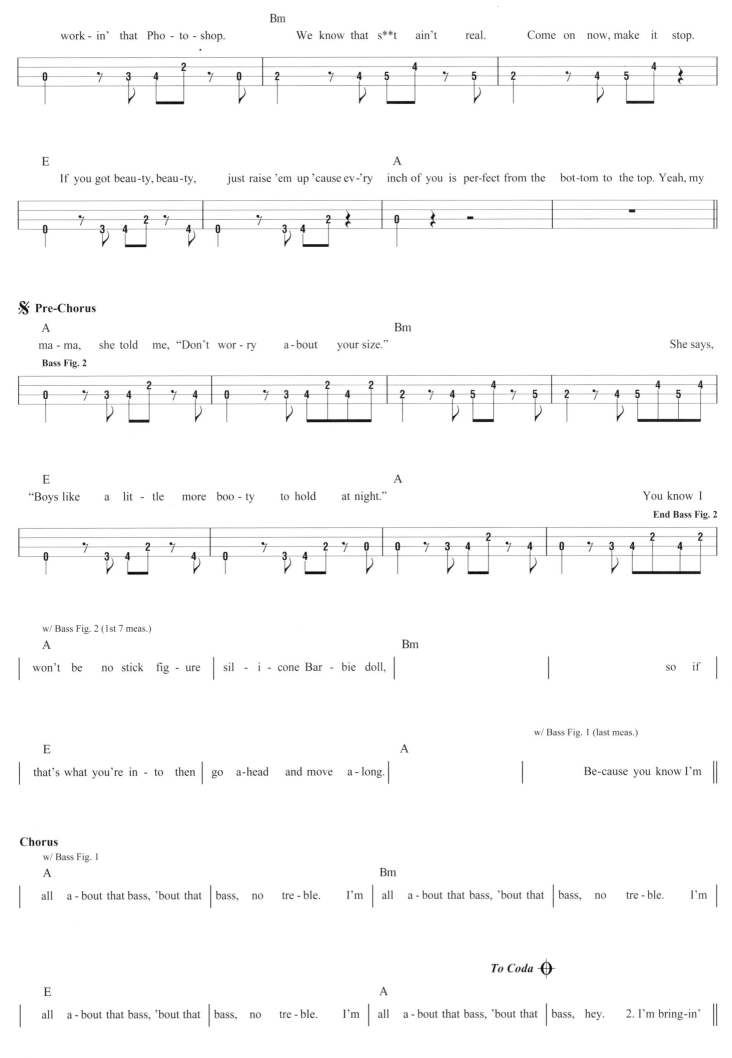

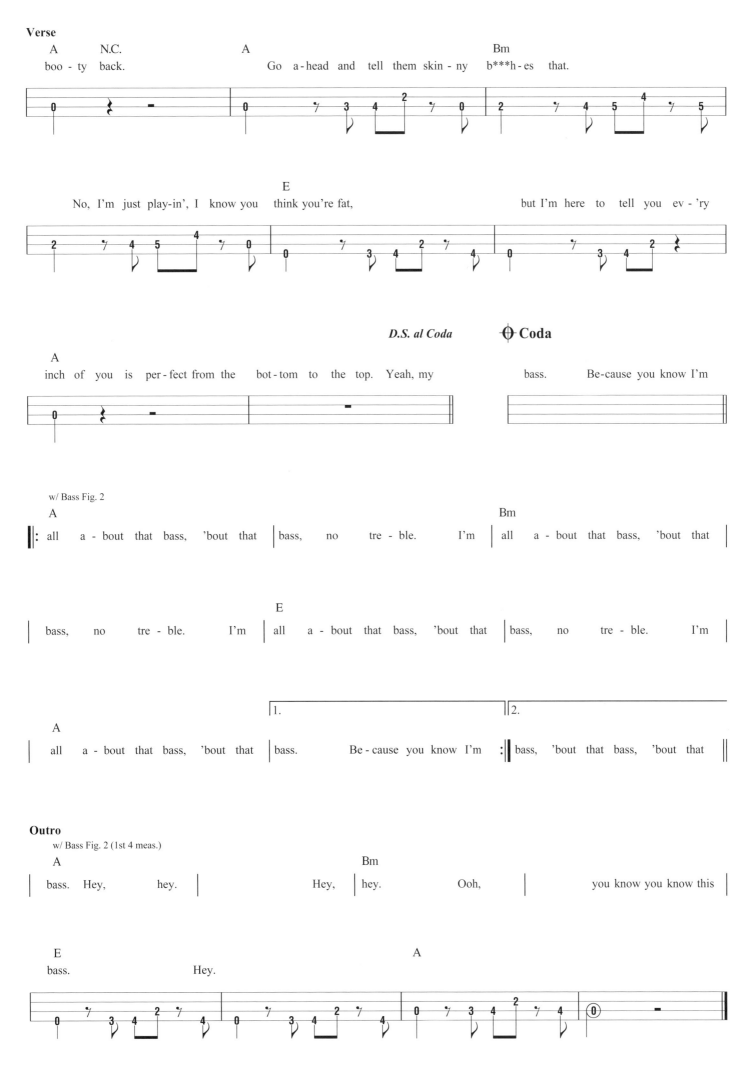

Africa

Words and Music by David Paich and Jeff Porcaro

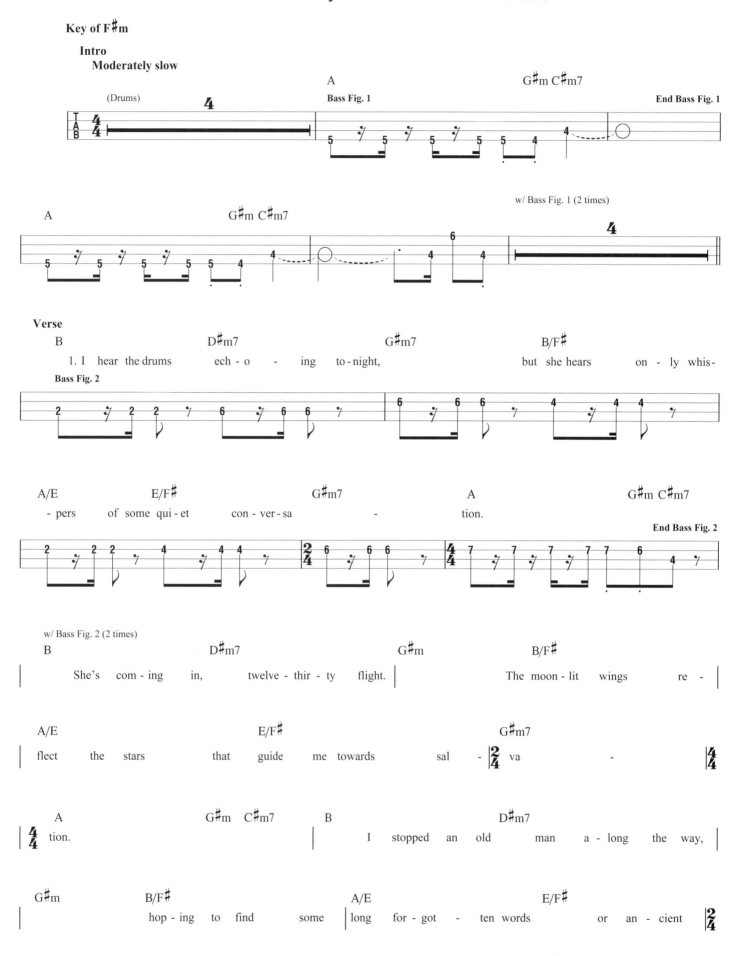

Key of F#m

Intro

Moderately slow

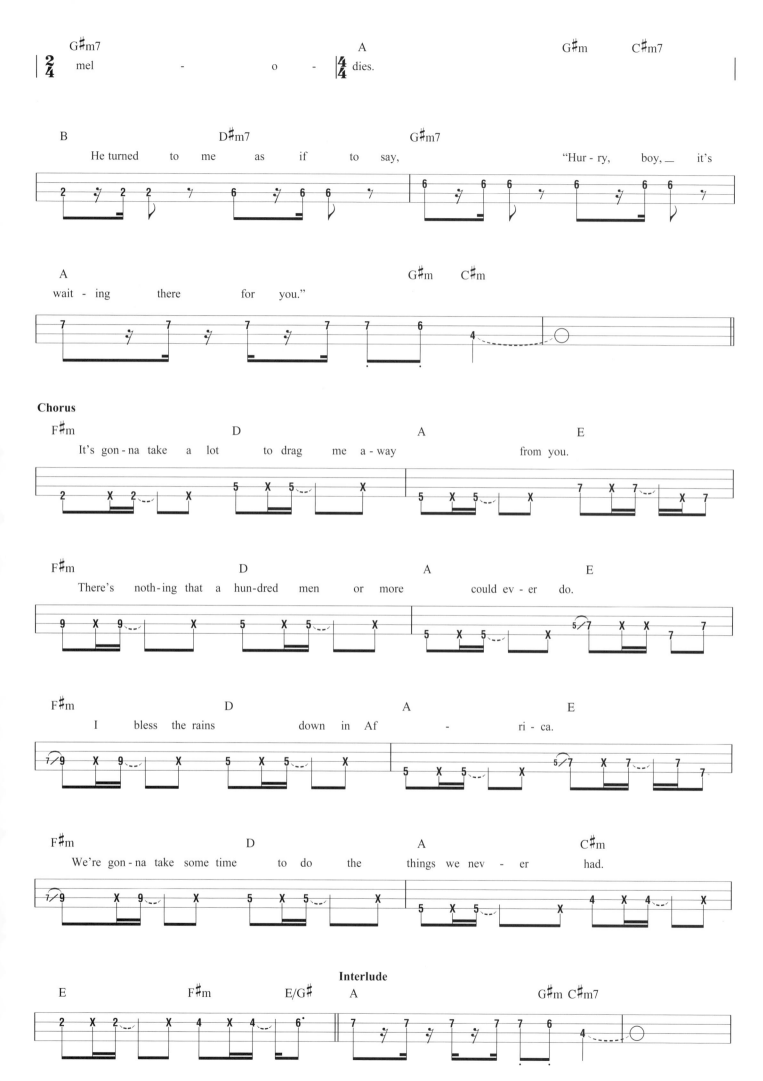

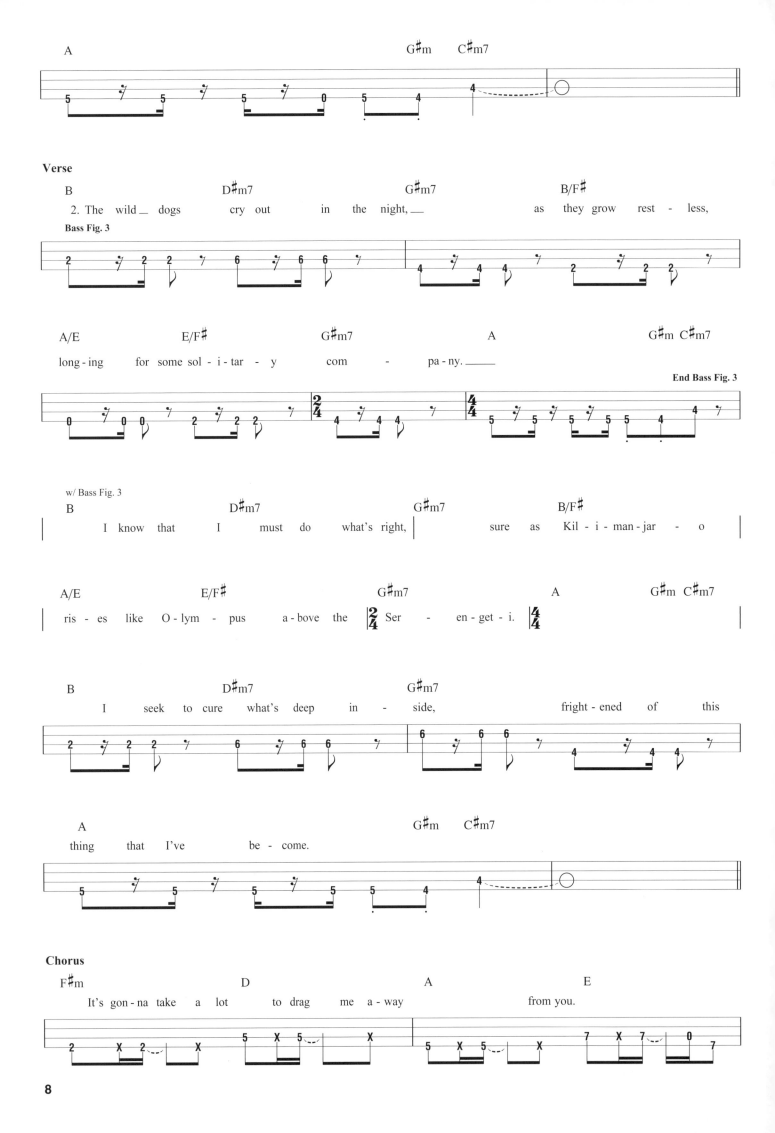

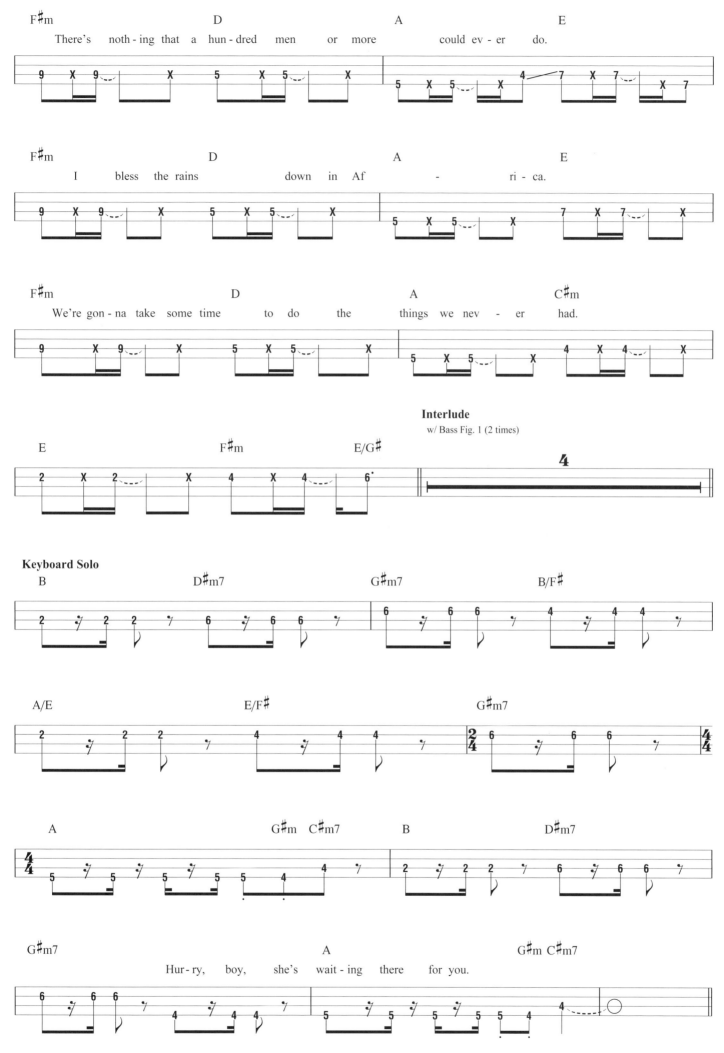

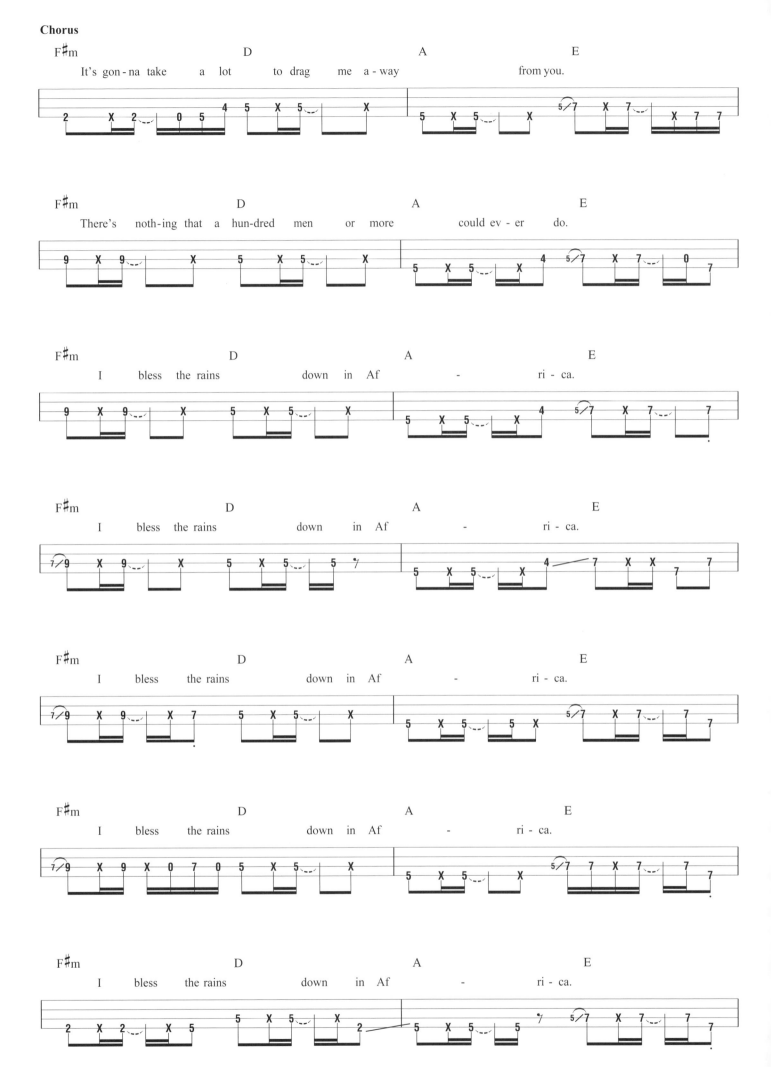

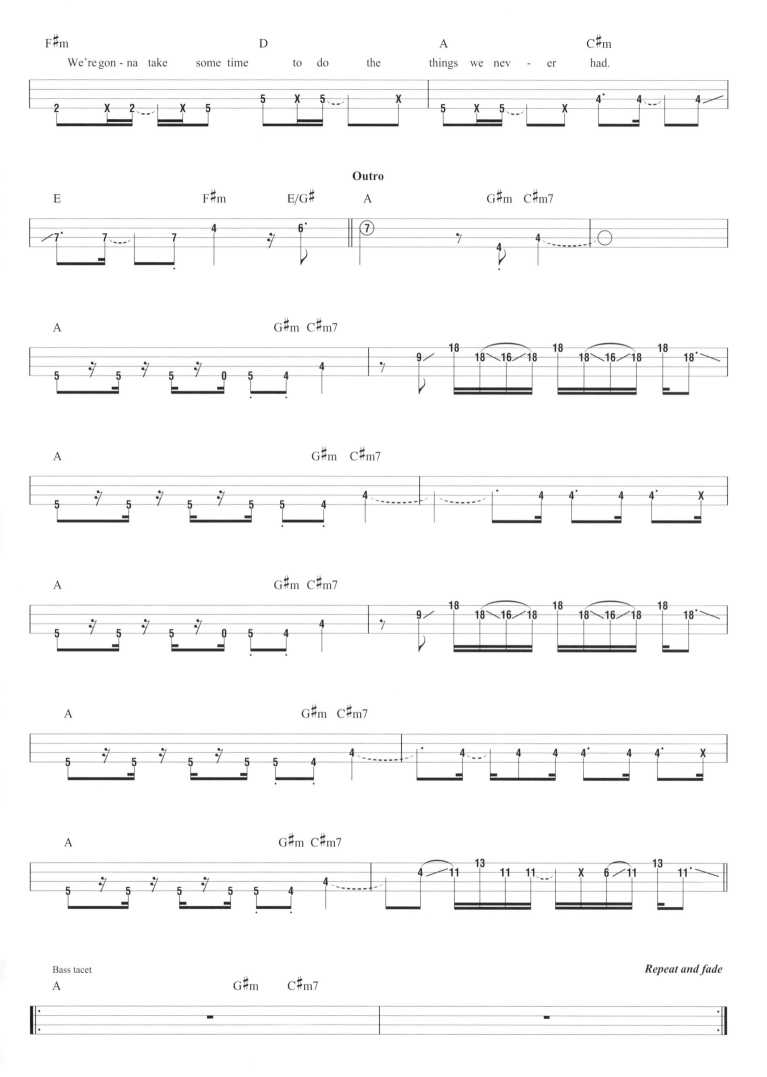

All Night Long (All Night)

Words and Music by Lionel Richie

5-string bass:
(low to high) B-E-A-D-G

Key of A♭

Intro
Moderately

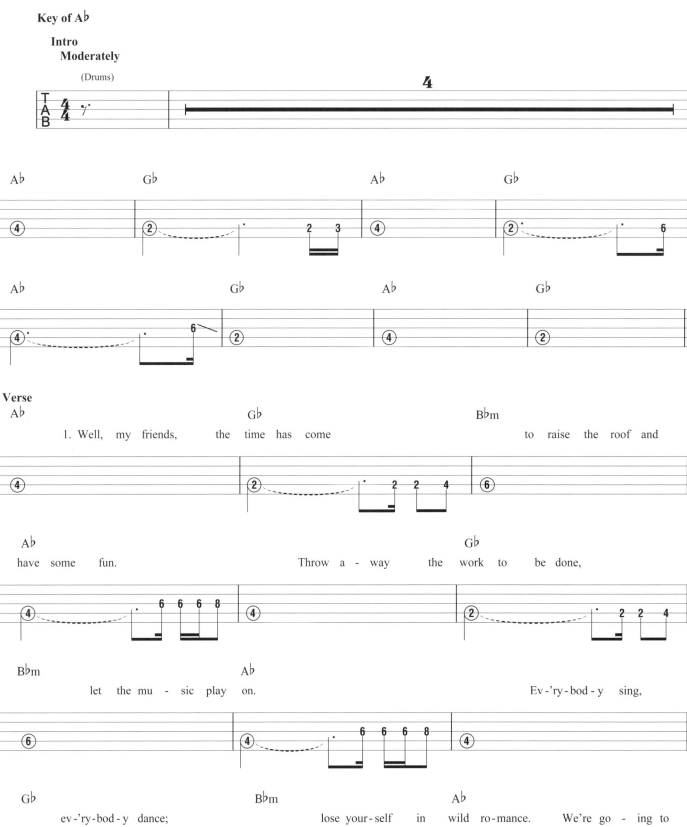

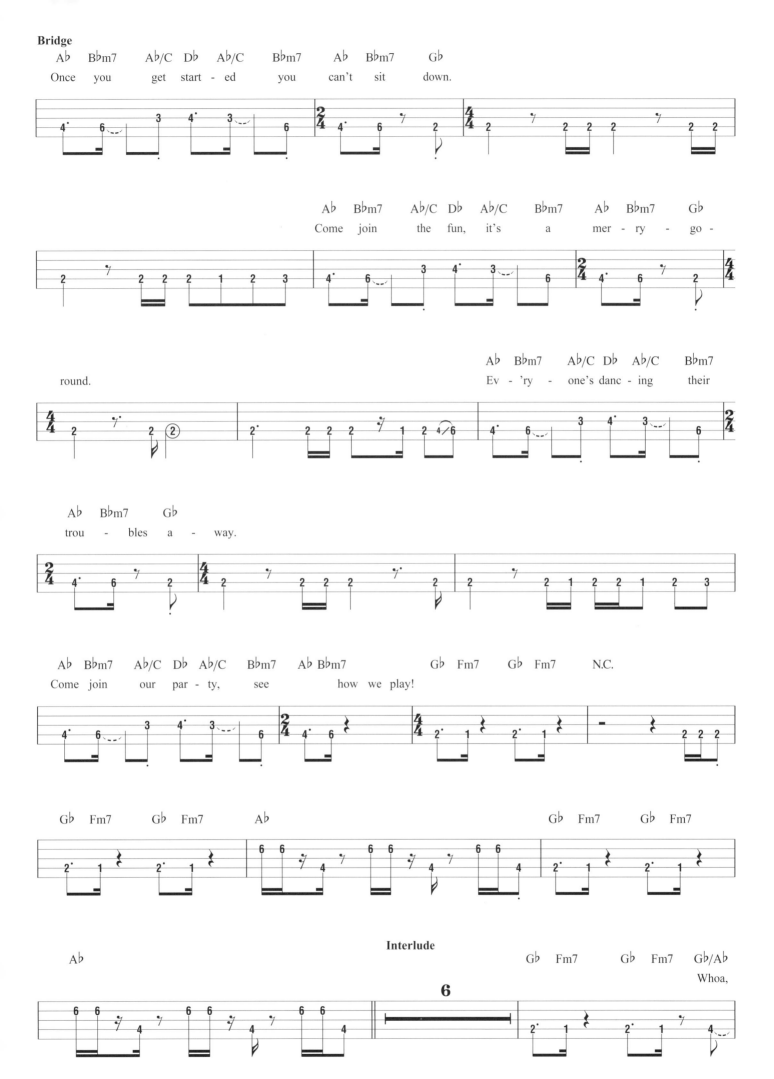

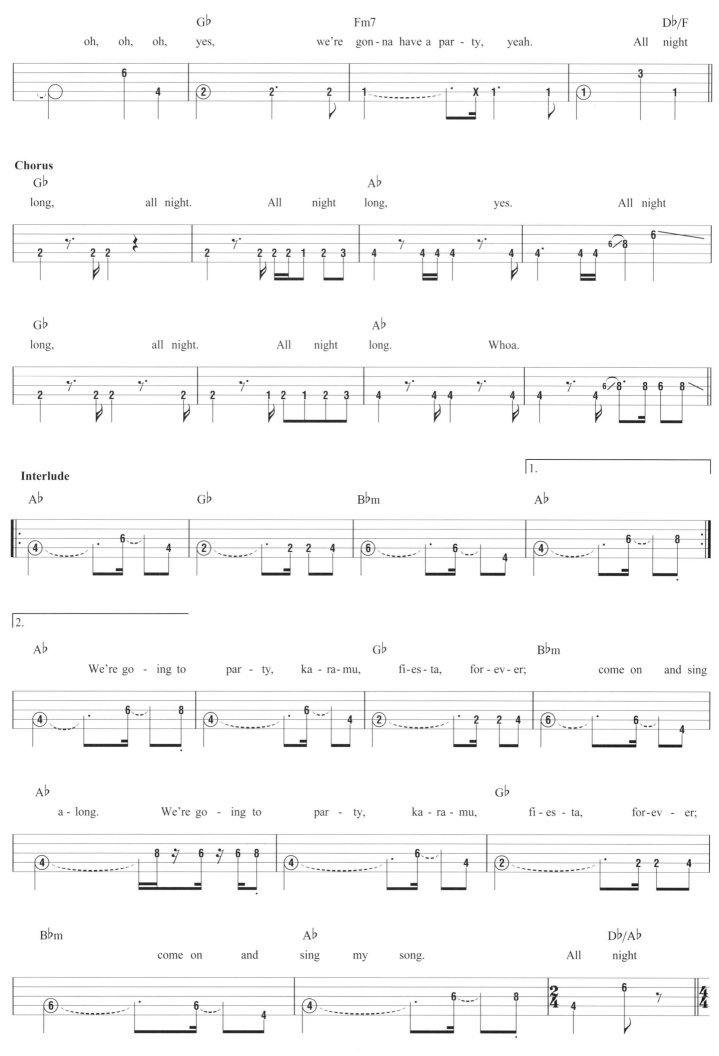

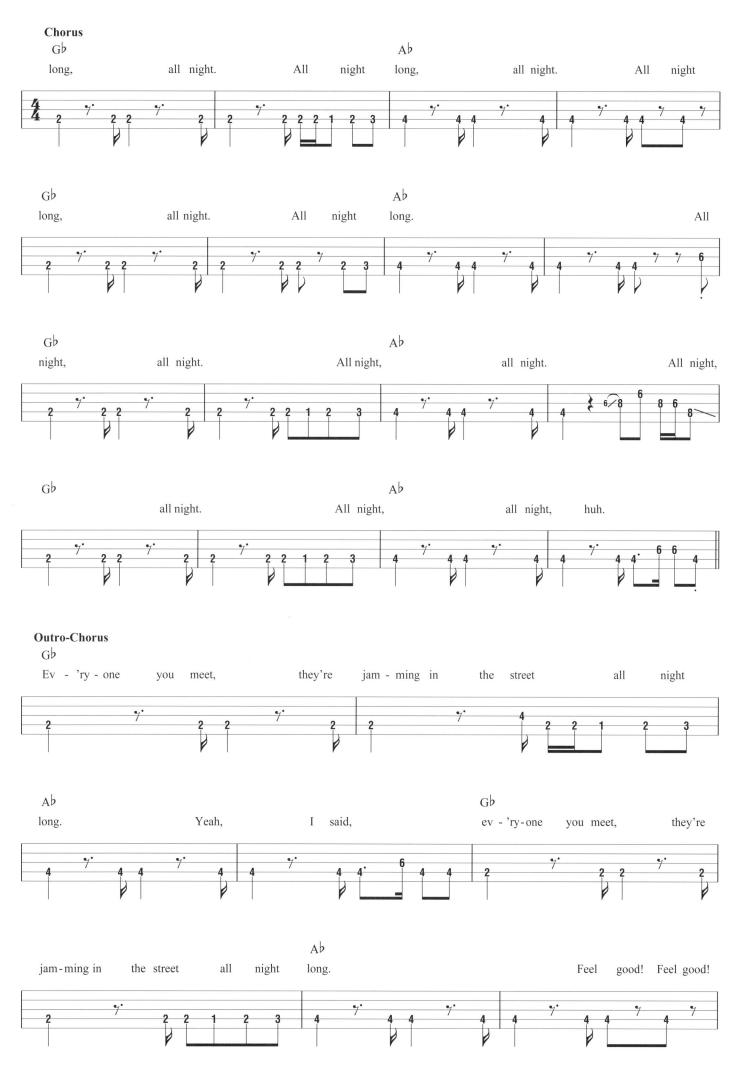

All Star

Words and Music by Greg Camp

Tune down 1/2 step:
(low to high) E♭-A♭-D♭-G♭

Key of G

Verse
Moderately

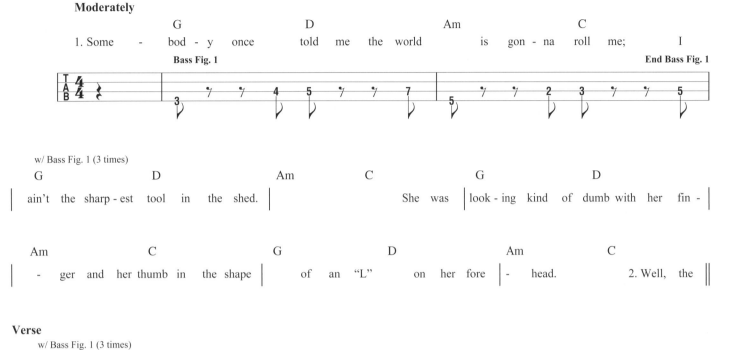

	G	D	Am	C
	1. Some - bod - y once told me the world		is gon - na roll me;	I

Bass Fig. 1   **End Bass Fig. 1**

w/ Bass Fig. 1 (3 times)

G	D	Am	C	G	D
ain't the sharp - est tool in the shed.		She was	look - ing kind of dumb with her fin -		

Am	C	G	D	Am	C
- ger and her thumb in the shape	of an "L" on her fore	- head.	2. Well, the

Verse

w/ Bass Fig. 1 (3 times)

G	D	Am	C
years start com - ing and they don't stop com - ing.	Fed to the rules, and I hit the ground run - ning.

3. *See additional lyrics*

G	D	Am	C
Did - n't make sense not to live for fun. Your	brain gets smart, but your head gets dumb.

G	D	Am	C
So much to do, so much to see. So what's wrong	with tak - ing the back streets? You'll

G	D	Am	C	F
nev - er know if you don't go. You'll nev - er shine if you don't glow.

Chorus

G	C	C♯m7♭5		C
Hey now, you're an all star; get your game on, go play.

Bass Fig. 2   **End Bass Fig. 2**

G	C	C#o	C

years start com-ing and they don't stop com-ing.   Fed   to the rules, and I hit the ground run-ning.

Bass Fig. 3   **End Bass Fig. 3**

w/ Bass Fig. 3 (2 times)

G	C	C#o	C

Did-n't make sense not to live for fun.   Your | brain gets smart, but your head gets dumb. |

G	C	C#o	C

So much to do, so much to see. So what's wrong | with tak - ing the back streets?   You'll |

G	C	C#o	C F

nev - er know if you don't go.   (Go!) You'll nev - er shine if you don't glow.

Chorus

w/ Bass Fig. 2 (5 times)

G	C	C#m7♭5	C	G	C

Hey now, you're an all star; get your | game on, go play. | Hey now, you're a rock star; get the |

C#m7♭5	C	G	C	C#m7♭5	C

show on, get paid. And | all that glit - ters is gold. | On - ly shoot - ing |

G C	C#m7♭5	C	G C	C#m7♭5	C

stars break the mold. | And | all that glit-ters is gold. | On - ly shoot-ing |

G	F	C

stars break the mold.

Additional Lyrics

3. It's a cool place, and they say it gets colder.
You're bundled up now; wait till you get older.
But the meteor men beg to differ,
Judging by the hole in the satellite picture.
The ice we skate is getting pretty thin.
The water's getting warm so you might as well swim.
My world's on fire. How 'bout yours?
That's the way I like it and I'll never get bored.

Attention

Words and Music by Charlie Puth and Jacob Kasher Hindlin

5-string bass:
(low to high) B-E-A-D-G

Key of E♭m

Intro
Moderately

Bass tacet

E♭m   D♭   B♭m7   C♭

4/4   Whoa.   Mmm.   1. You've been

Verse

E♭m   D♭
run - nin' 'round, run - nin' 'round, run - nin' 'round, throw - in' that | dirt all on my name 'cause you

B♭m7   C♭
knew that I, knew that I, knew that I'd call you | up.   You've been

E♭m   D♭
go - in' 'round, go - in' 'round, go - in' 'round ev - er - y | par - ty in L. A. 'cause you

B♭m7   C♭
knew that I, knew that I, knew that I'd be at | one.

Pre-Chorus

E♭m   D♭   B♭m7
I know that dress is kar - ma, per - fume re - gret. You got me think - in' 'bout when you were mine.

TAB: ⑥   ④   ①

C♭   E♭m   D♭
Ooh.   And now I'm all up on you; what you ex - pect? But

TAB: ②   ⑥   ④

B♭m7   C♭   N.C.
you're not com - ing home with me to - night. You just want at -

TAB: ①   ②

Chorus

E♭m   D♭
ten - tion, you don't want my heart. May - be you just

Bass Fig. 1

TAB:
4 - 6 - 7 - 4 - 6 - - 4 - 6 - 7 - - 4 - 7 - 2 - 4 - 7 - - 4 - 3 - 2
4 - - - - X - 4 - - - 2 - - - - - - 2 - - - -

Bbm7　　　　　　　　　　　　　　　　　**Gb**　　**Cb**　　　　　　　　　　　　　　**Db**

hate the　　thought of　　me with　some - one　new.　　　　　Yeah, you　just want at -

End Bass Fig. 1

```
|--------1.---------3.----------1--3--------3.------------|---------------4----3--4------4--------6-----|
|---1.------------.7.-----------------------------4------|---2.----------.7.-------------2------4------|
|--------------------------------------------2-----------|-------------------------------------------- |
```

To Coda ⊕

w/ Bass Fig. 1

Ebm　　　　　　　　　　　　　**Db**　　　　　　　　　**Bbm7**　　　　　　　**Gb**

ten - tion,　　I knew from the　｜start.　　　You're just mak - ing　｜sure I'm　nev - er　get - ting　o - ver

Verse
w/ Bass Fig. 1 (2 times)

Cb　　　　　　　　　　　**Db**　　　　　**Ebm**

｜you.　　　　　　2. You've been　‖run - nin''round,　run - nin''round,　run - nin''round,　throw - in'　that　｜

Db　　　　　　　　　　　　　　**Bbm7**　　　　　　　　　　　　　**Gb**

｜dirt　all　on　my　name　'cause you　｜knew that　I,　knew that　I,　knew that　I'd　call　you　｜

Cb　　　　　　　　　　　**Db**　　　　　**Ebm**

｜up.　　　　　　　　　Ba - by,　｜now　that we're,　now　that we're,　now　that we're　right　here　｜

Db　　　　　　　　　　　　　　**Bbm7**　　　　　　　　　**Gb**　　**Cb**　　　　　**Db**

｜stand - ing face　to　face,　　　you al -　｜read - y know, read - y know, read - y know that you　｜won.　　Oh.　　　　‖

Pre-Chorus
w/ Bass Fig. 1

Ebm

｜　　　I know　that　dress　is　kar - ma,　｜　　per - fume　re - gret.　　　　You　｜

D.S. al Coda

Bbm7　　　　　　　　　　　**Gb**　　**Cb**　　　　　　　　　　　**Db**

｜got me think - in' 'bout　when you　were mine.　｜got me think - in' 'bout　when you　were mine.)　‖

⊕ **Coda**

Bridge
w/ Bass Fig. 1 (2 times)

Cb　　　　**Db**　　**Ebm**　　　　　　　　　　　　　**Db**

｜you.　　Oh.　　　‖　What　are you do - ing　to me? What　｜are you do - ing, huh?
　　　　　　　　　　　　　　　　　　　　　　　　　　　　　　(What are you do -

Bbm7　　　　　　　　　　　**Gb**　　**Cb**　　　　　　　　　　　**Db**

｜　　What　are you　do - ing　to me? What　｜are you　do - ing, huh?
｜ - ing?　　　　　　　　　　　　　　　　　　　　　　　What are you do -

E♭m		**D♭**		**B♭m7**		**G♭**

What are you do-ing to me? What | are you do-ing, huh? | What are you do-ing to me? What
-ing? | What are you do | -ing?)

Pre-Chorus
Bass tacet

C♭		**D♭**	**E♭m**

are you do - ing, huh? ‖ I know that dress is kar - ma,

D♭		**B♭m7**		**C♭**

per - fume re - gret. You | got me think - in' 'bout when you were mine.

E♭m		**D♭**

And now I'm all up on you; what you ex - pect? But

⑥   ④

B♭m7		**C♭**	**N.C.**

you're not com - ing home with me to - night. You just want at -

①   ②   -   -

Outro-Chorus
w/ Bass Fig. 1 (4 times)

E♭m		**D♭**		**B♭m7**		**G♭**

ten - tion, you don't want my | heart. May - be you just | hate the thought of me with some - one

C♭		**D♭**	**E♭m**

new. Yeah, you just want at - | ten - tion, I knew from the

D♭		**B♭m7**		**G♭**	**C♭**		**D♭**

start. You're just mak - ing | sure I'm nev - er get-ting o - ver | you.

E♭m		**D♭**

(What are you do - ing to me? What | are you do - ing, huh?

B♭m7		**G♭**	**C♭**		**D♭**

What are you do - ing to me? What | are you do - ing, huh?) Yeah, you just want at -

E♭m		**D♭**

ten - tion, I knew from the | start. You're just mak - ing

Bass tacet

B♭m7		**G♭**	**C♭**		**D♭**	**E♭5**

sure I'm nev - er get - ting o - ver | you.

24

Bad Guy

Words and Music by Billie Eilish O'Connell and Finneas O'Connell

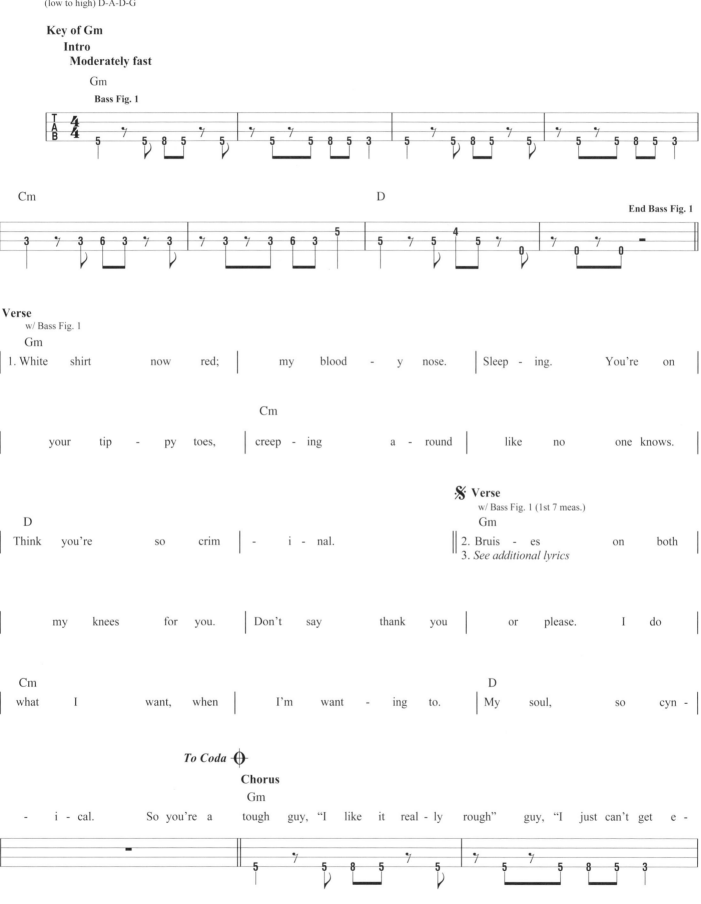

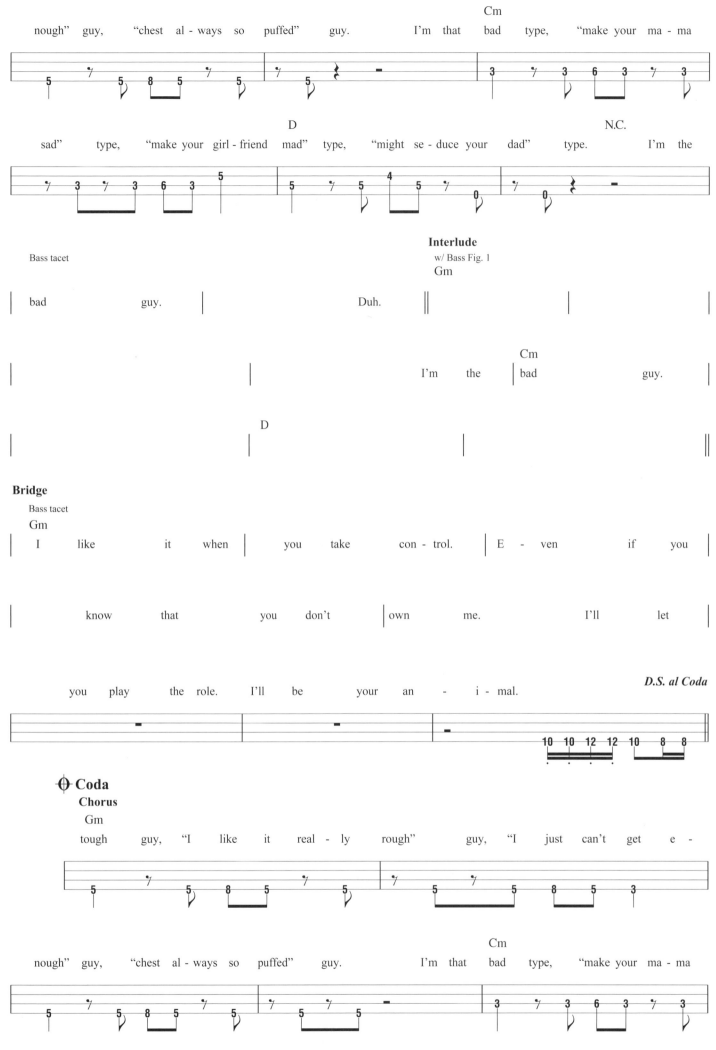

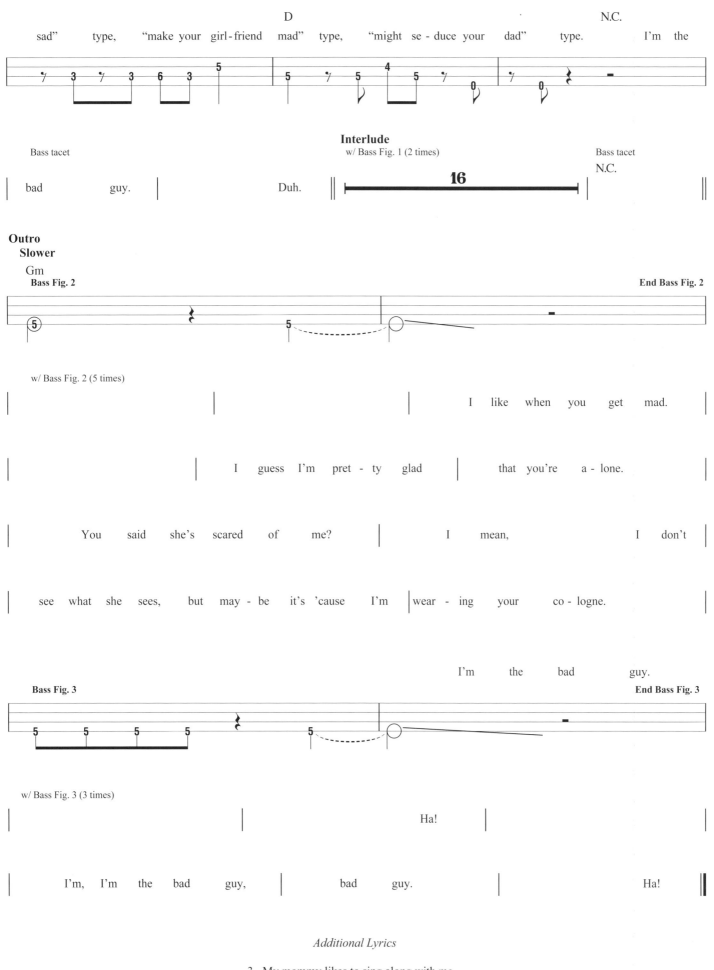

Beat It

Words and Music by Michael Jackson

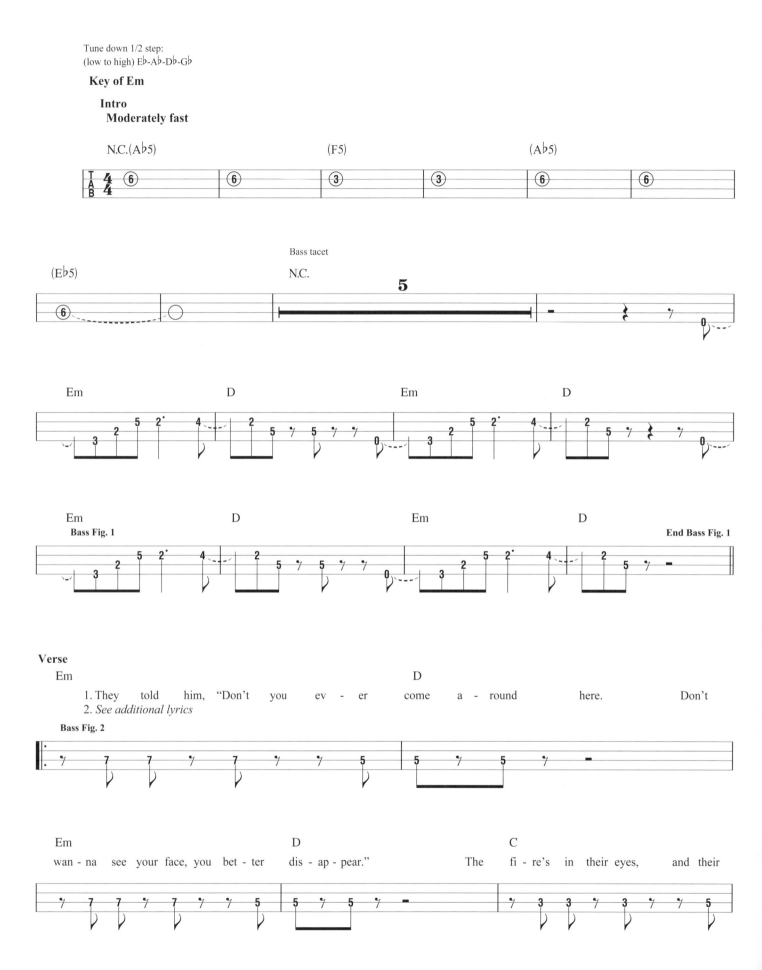

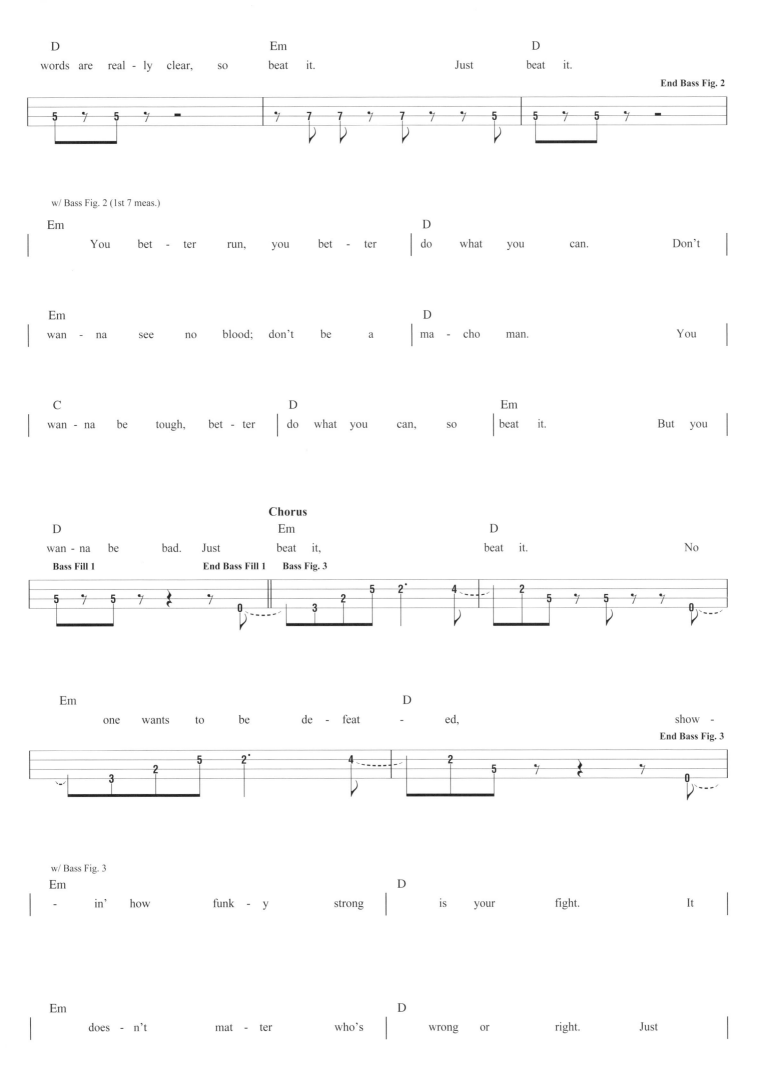

1.

w/ Bass Fig. 1

Em	D	Em	D
beat it.	Just	beat it.	Just	beat it.	Just	beat it.	Oh!

2.

w/ Bass Fig. 3

Em	D	Em
beat it,	beat it.	No	one wants to be de-feat-

w/ Bass Fig. 1

D	Em	D
ed,	show	- in' how funk-y strong	is your fight.	It

Em	D
does - n't mat - ter who's	wrong or right.	Just

Interlude

N.C.(E5)

beat it.   Beat it.

Bass Fig. 4   End Bass Fig. 4

w/ Bass Fig. 4 (6 times)

Beat it.

Beat it.

Beat it.

Guitar Solo

w/ Bass Fig. 2 (1 7/8 times)   w/ Bass Fill 1

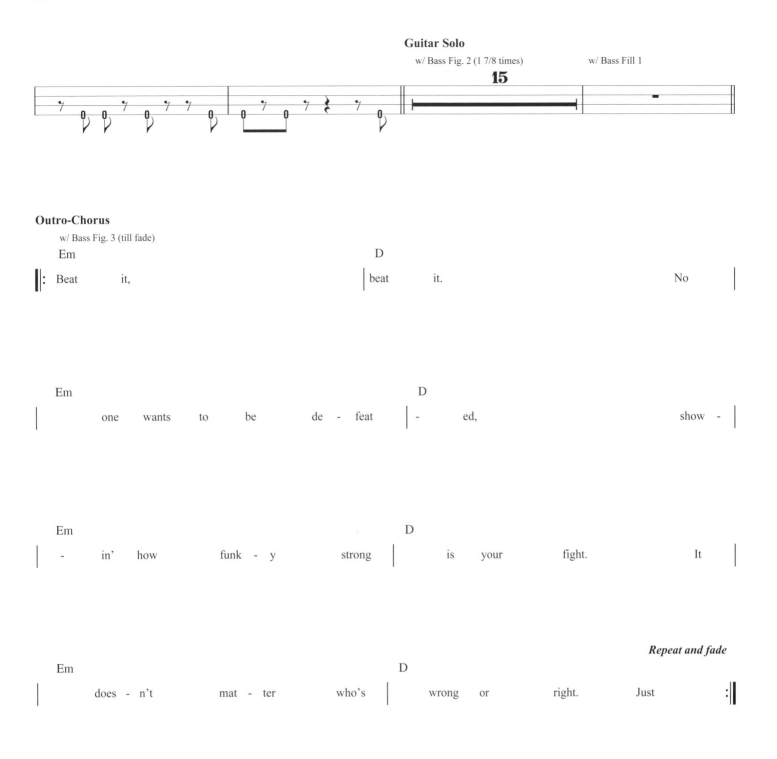

Outro-Chorus

w/ Bass Fig. 3 (till fade)

Em   D

Beat   it,   beat   it.   No

Em   D

one   wants   to   be   de - feat | - ed,   show -

Em   D

- in'   how   funk - y   strong | is   your   fight.   It

Repeat and fade

Em   D

does - n't   mat - ter   who's | wrong   or   right.   Just

Additional Lyrics

2. They're out to get you, better leave while you can.
   Don't wanna be a boy, you wanna be a man.
   You wanna stay alive, better do what you can, so beat it. Just beat it.
   You have to show them that you're really not scared.
   You're playing with your life, this ain't no truth or dare.
   They'll kick you then they beat you then they'll tell you it's fair, so beat it.
   But you wanna be bad.

Beautiful Day

Words by Bono
Music by U2

Key of D

Intro
Moderately fast

Bass tacet

1. The heart is a bloom,

Verse

A   Bm   D   G

shoots

Bass Fig. 1

D   A

up   through the ston - y   ground.   But there's no room,

End Bass Fig. 1

w/ Bass Fig. 1 (5 times)

A   Bm   D   G   D   A

no space to rent in this town.

Bm   D   G

You're out of luck,   and the

D   A   Bm   D

rea - son that you had to care.   The traf - fic is stuck,

G   D   A

and you're not mov - ing an - y - where.

Bm   D   G

You thought you'd found a friend   to take you

D   A   Bm   D

out of this place,   some - one you could lend

G   D   A

a hand in re - turn for grace.   It's a beau - ti - ful day.

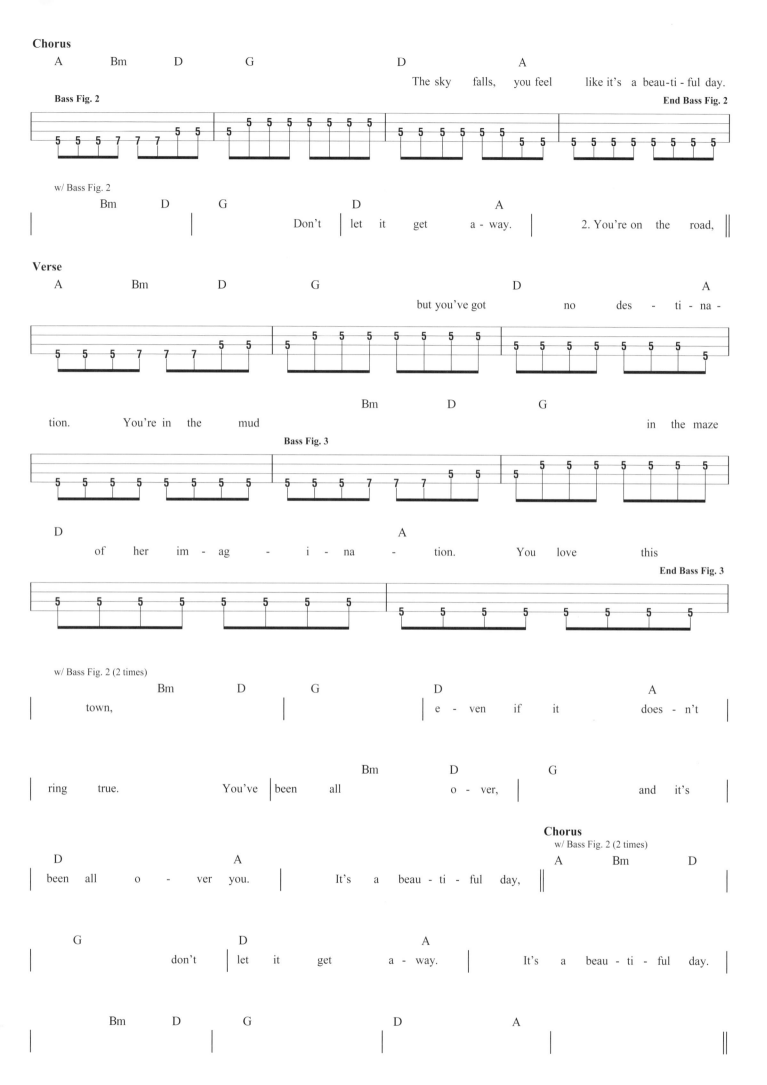

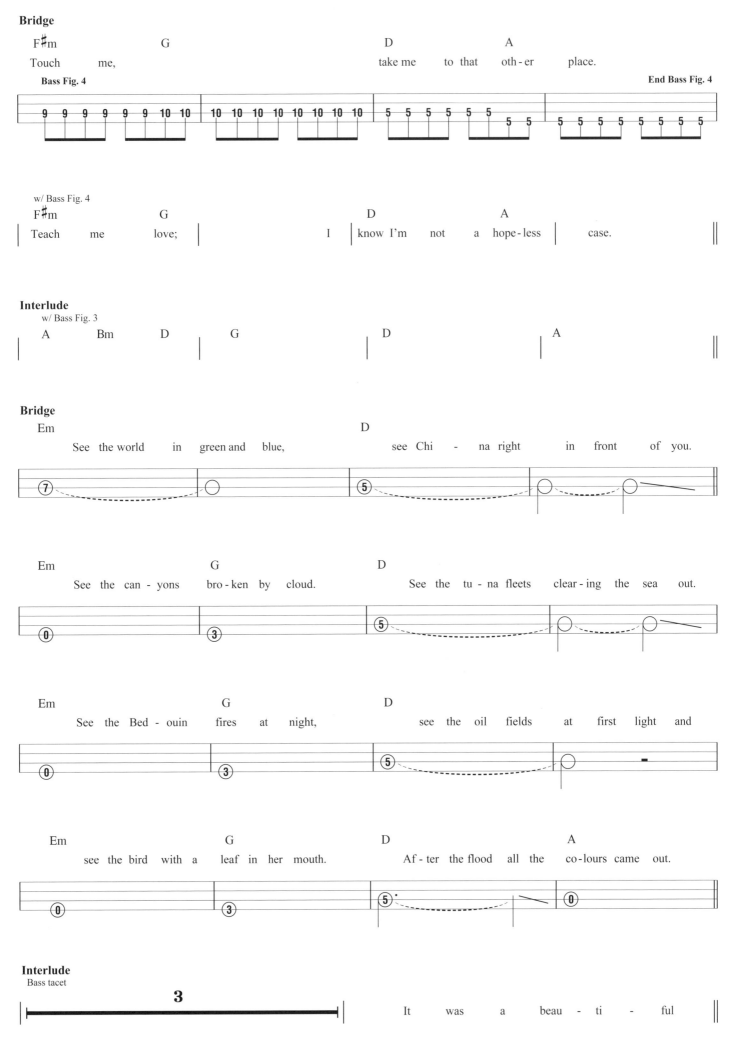

Bridge

F#m   G   D   A

Touch   me,   take me   to that   oth - er   place.

Bass Fig. 4   **End Bass Fig. 4**

w/ Bass Fig. 4

F#m   G   D   A

Teach   me   love;   I   know I'm   not   a   hope - less   case.

Interlude

w/ Bass Fig. 3

A   Bm   D   G   D   A

Bridge

Em   D

See the world   in   green and   blue,   see Chi - na right   in   front   of   you.

Em   G   D

See the can - yons   bro - ken by   cloud.   See the tu - na fleets   clear - ing   the   sea   out.

Em   G   D

See the Bed - ouin   fires   at   night,   see the oil fields   at   first   light and

Em   G   D   A

see the bird   with a   leaf in   her   mouth.   Af - ter the flood   all   the   co - lours came   out.

Interlude

Bass tacet

3

It   was   a   beau - ti - ful

Chorus

w/ Bass Fig. 2 (2 times)

| A | Bm | D | G | | D | | A | |
| day. | | | | Don't | let it get a - way. | | Beau - ti - ful | |

| A | Bm | D | G | | D | | A | |
| day. | | | | | | | | |

Bridge

w/ Bass Fig. 4

F#m   G   D   A

Touch me,   take me to that oth - er place.

F#m   G   D   A

Reach me; I know I'm not a hope - less case. What you

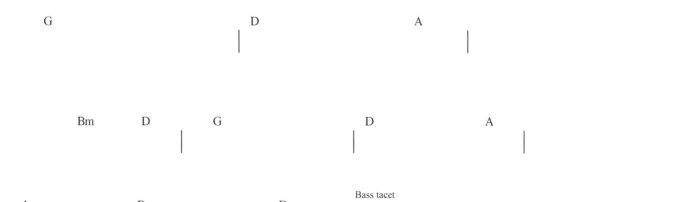

Outro

w/ Bass Fig. 2 (4 times)

A   Bm   D   G   D   A

don't have you don't   need it now,   what you don't know you can feel

           Bm   D   G

it some - how. What you don't have you don't   need it now,   don't

D   A   Bm   D

need it now.   It's a beau - ti - ful day.

G   D   A

Bm   D   G   D   A

A   Bm   D   Bass tacet

Beggin'

Words and Music by Bob Gaudio and Peggy Farina

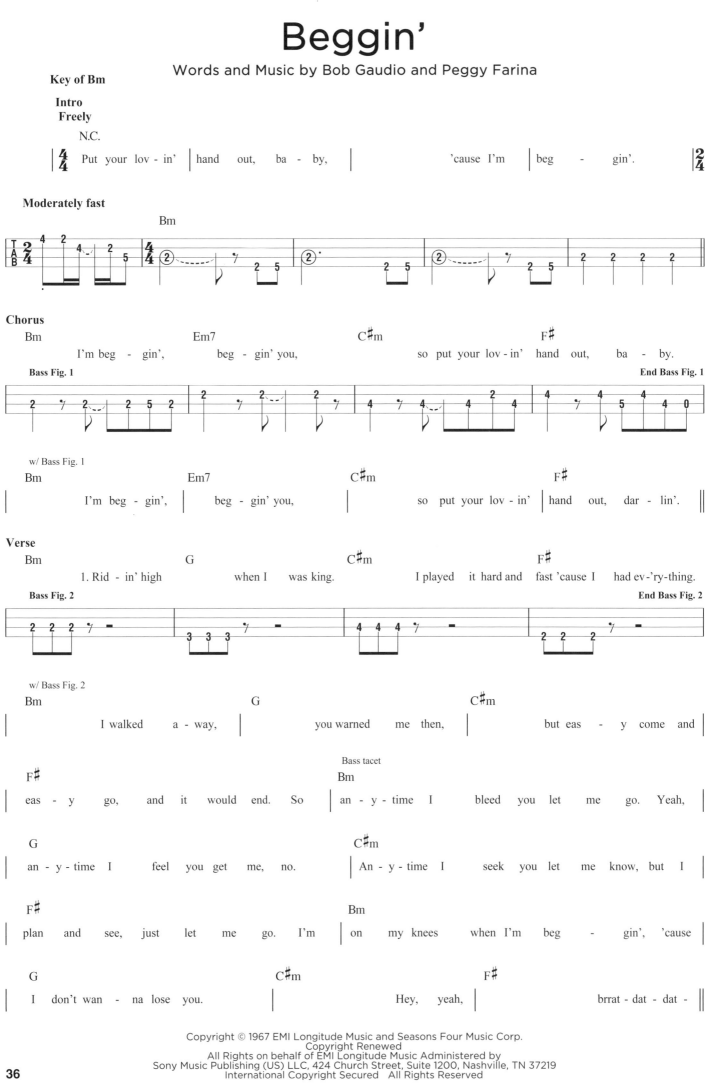

Chorus

w/ Bass Fig. 1 (2 times)

| Bm | Em7 | C#m | F# |

| dah. 'Cause I'm beg - gin', | beg - gin' you, | and put your lov - in' | hand out, ba - by. |

| Bm | Em7 | C#m | F# |

| I'm beg - gin', | beg - gin' you, | and put your lov - in' | hand out, dar - lin'. |

Verse

| N.C.(Bm) | G | C#m7 | F# |

2. I need you to un - der-stand: tried so hard to be your man,

Bass Fig. 3

| Bm | G | C#m7 | F# |

the kind of man you want in the end. On - ly then can I be - gin to live a-gain.

End Bass Fig. 3

w/ Bass Fig. 2 (2 times)

| Bm | G | C#m |

| An emp - ty shell | I used to be. | The shad - ow of my |

| F# | Bm | G |

| life was hang - in' o - ver me. | A bro - ken man | that I don't know, |

| C#m | F# |

| won't e - ven stand the | dev - il's chance to win my soul. What we |

Bridge

w/ Bass Fig. 1 (3 times)

| Bm | Em7 |

| do - in'? What we chas - in'? Why the | bot - tom? Why the base - ment? Why we |

| C#m | F# |

| got good s**t, don't em - brace it? Why the | feel for the need to re - place me? You're the |

| Bm | Em7 |

| wrong - way track from the good. I wan - na paint a | pic - ture tell - in' where we could be at. Lov - in' |

| C#m | F# |

| heart in the best way it should. You can give it a - | way, you have, and you took the bait. But I |

| Bm | Em7 |

| keep walk - in' on, keep o - pen - in' doors, | keep hop - in' for that the door is yours. |

| C#m | F# |

| Keep al - so home, 'cause I don't wan - na | live in a bro - ken home, girl, I'm beg - gin'. |

37

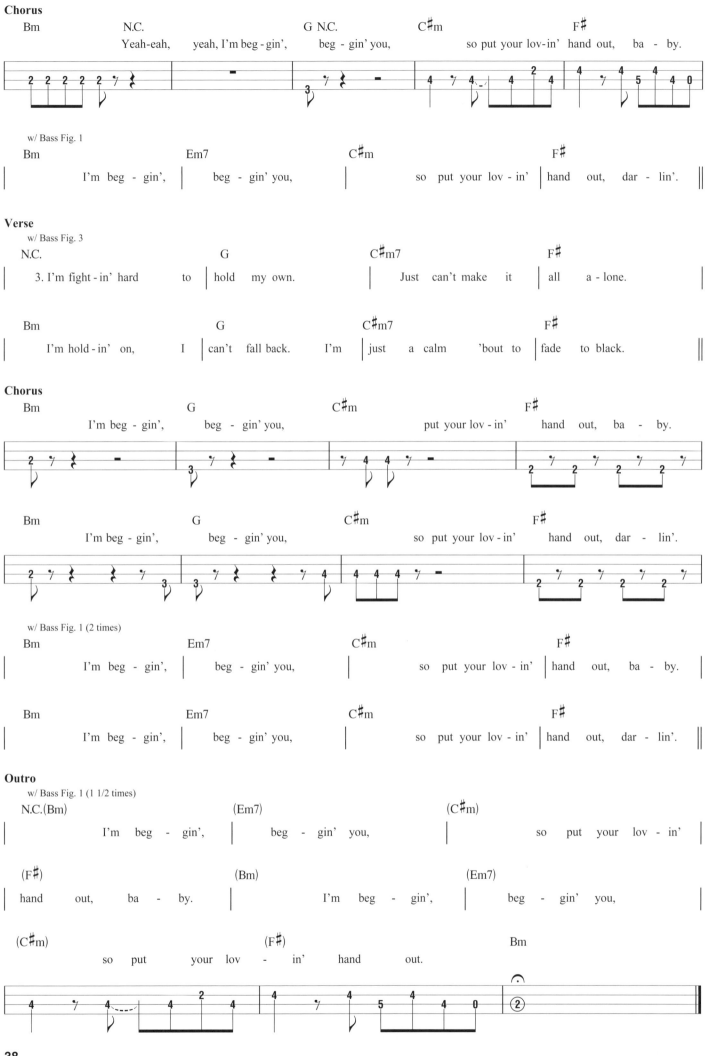

Can't Feel My Face

Words and Music by Abel Tesfaye, Max Martin, Savan Kotecha, Anders Svensson and Ali Payami

Key of Am

Intro
Moderately

G   F   Am

1. And I know

Bass Fig. 1   **End Bass Fig. 1**

Verse

w/ Bass Fig. 1 (2 times)

G

she'll be the death of me, at least | we'll both be numb. And she'll al-

Am

-ways get the best of me, the worst | is yet to come. But at least

G

we'll both be beau-ti-ful and stay | for-ev-er young. This I know,

Pre-Chorus
w/ Bass Fig. 1

Am   G

this I know. | She told me, "Don't || wor-ry a-bout

F   Am

it." She told me, "Don't | wor-ry no more." | We both know we

G   F

can't go with-out it. She told me, "You'll

Am   N.C.

nev-er be a-lo-o-one." Oo.

Chorus

G   F

I can't feel my face when I'm with you, but I love

Bass Fig. 2

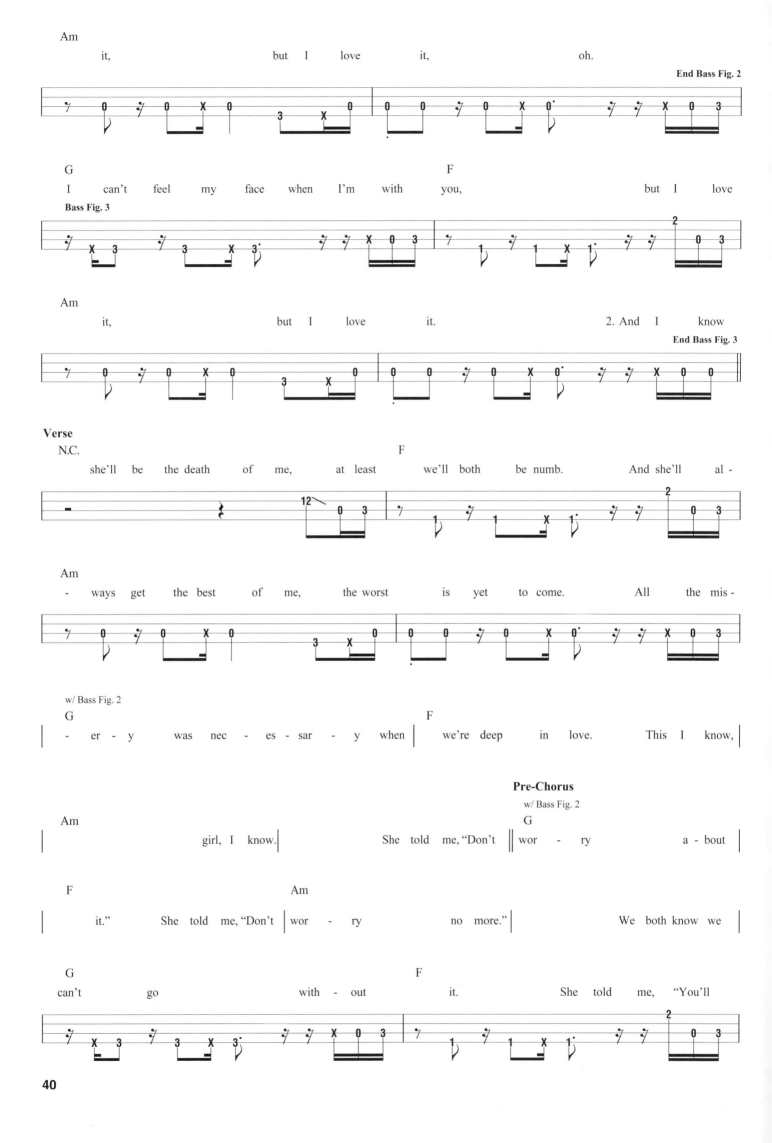

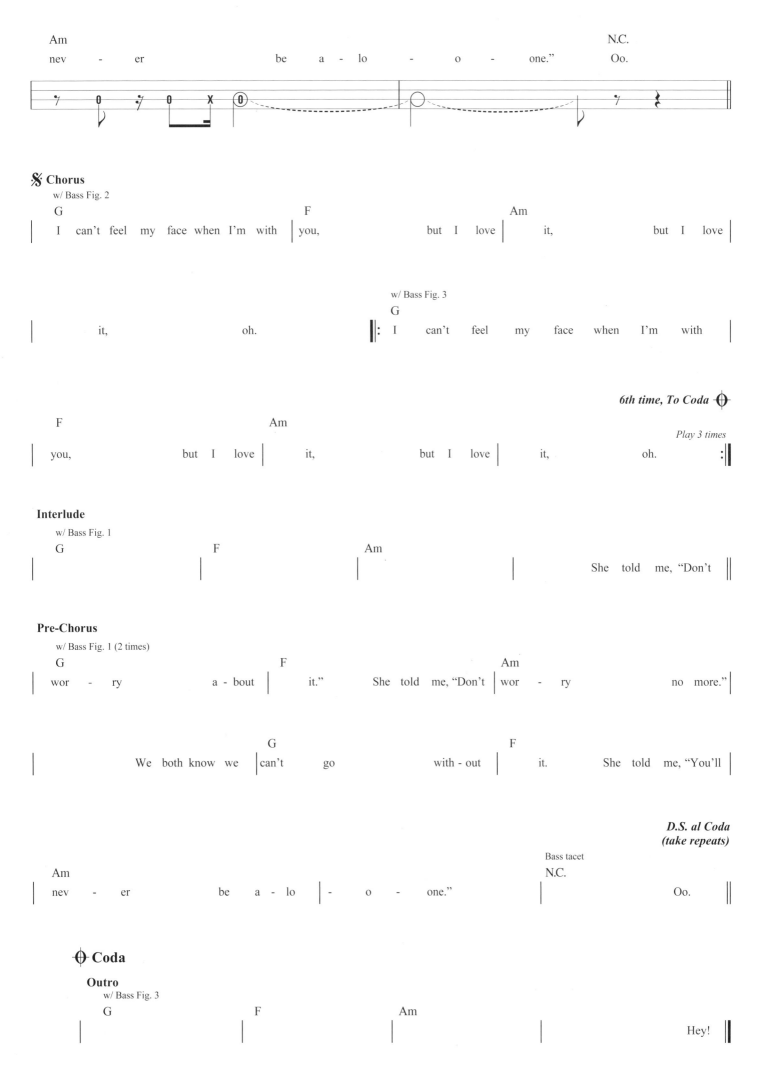

41

Circles

Words and Music by Austin Post, Kaan Gunesberk, Louis Bell, William Walsh and Adam Feeney

Key of C

Intro
Moderately fast

w/ Bass Fig. 1

| Cmaj7 | Em7/B | Fmaj7 | G ||

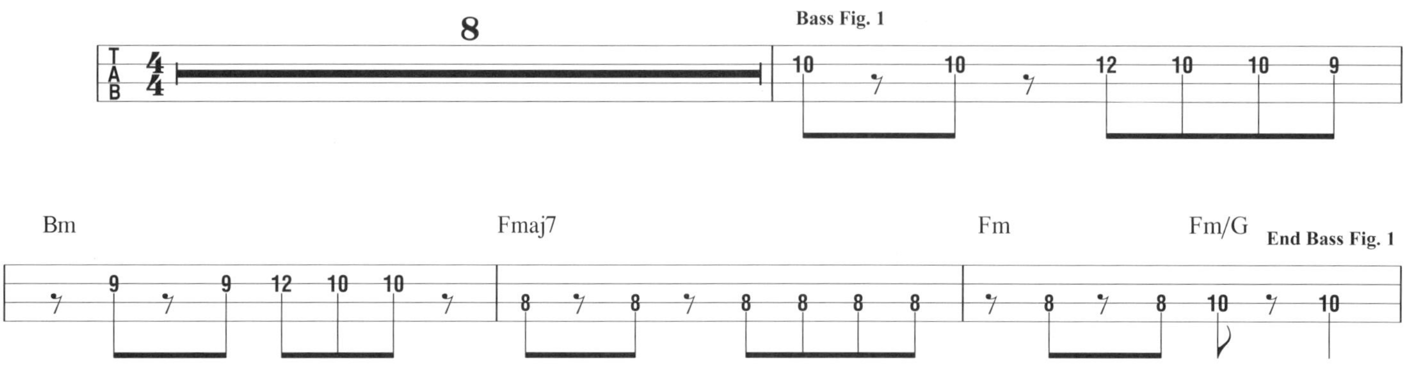

Verse

w/ Bass Fig. 1 (4 times)

| C | G/B 1. We could - n't turn a - round | F |

| Fm 'til we were Fm/G up - side down. | C | G/B I'll be the bad guy now, |

| F | but no, I G ain't too proud. | Cmaj7 |

| Em7/B I could - n't be there. | Fmaj7 | Fm E - ven Fm/G when I try, |

| Cmaj7 | Em7/B you don't be - lieve it. | Fmaj7 | N.C. We do this ev - 'ry time. ||

Chorus

w/ Bass Fig. 1 (4 times)

| Cmaj7 Sea - sons changed and our | Em7/B love went cold. | Fmaj7 Feed the flame 'cause we |

| F/G   Cmaj7   Em7/B
| can't let go. | Run a - way, but we're | run - ning in cir - cles. |

| Fmaj7   G   Cmaj7
| Run a - way,   run | a - way.   I dare you to do | some - thing. |

| Em7/B   Fmaj7   Fm   F/G
| I'm wait - ing on you | a - gain | so I don't take the blame. |

| Cmaj7   Em7/B   Fmaj7   G
| Run a - way, but we're | run - ning in cir - cles. | Run a - way,   run | a - way,   run a - way. ‖

Verse

      C   G/B   F   G N.C.
  2. Let   go,   I got a feel - ing that it's time to let   go.   I

w/ Bass Fig. 1 (2 times)
      C   G/B   F
| say   so. | I knew that this was doomed | from the get - go. |

                          F/G   Cmaj7
| You thought that   it   was | spe - cial,   spe - |

| G/B   Fmaj7   Fm   Fm/G
| cial,   but it was just the | sex, oh,   the sex | though.   And I still hear the |

| Cmaj7   Em7/B   Fmaj7   N.C.
| ech - oes;   I got a feel - ing that it's time to let it go.   Let it go.

𝄋 Chorus

1st time, w/ Bass Fig. 1 (4 times)
2nd time, w/ Bass Fig. 1 (2 times)
| Cmaj7   Em7/B   Fmaj7
| Sea - sons change   and our | love went   cold. | Feed the flame 'cause we |

| F/G   Cmaj7   Em7/B
| can't let go. | Run a - way, but we're | run - ning in cir - cles. |

43

To Coda ⊕

Fmaj7 / G / Cmaj7
Run a - way, run | a - way. I dare you to do | some - thing. |

Em7/B / Fmaj7 / Fm / F/G
I'm wait - ing on you | a - gain | so I don't take the blame. |

Cmaj7 / Em7/B / Fmaj7
Run a - way, but we're | run - ning in cir - cles. | Run a - way, run |

Bridge
Bass tacet
G / Cmaj7 / Bm
a - way, run a - way. ‖ May - be you don't un - der - | stand what I'm go - ing through. |

F / Fm / Cmaj7
It's on - ly me; | what you got to lose? | Make up your mind. Tell me, |

D.S. al Coda

G/B / Fmaj7 / N.C.
what are you gon - na do? | It's on - ly me. | Let it go. ‖

⊕ **Coda**

Cmaj7 / Em7/B
some - thing. I'm wait - ing on you

Fmaj7 / Fm / F/G
a - gain so I don't take the blame.

Bass tacet
Cmaj7 / Em7/B
Run a - way, but we're | run - ning in cir - cles. |

Fmaj7 / G / C / N.C.
Run a - way, run | a - way, run a - way. |

44

Come on Eileen

Words and Music by Kevin Rowland, James Patterson and Kevin Adams

Key of F

Intro

Moderately fast   **Moderately**

Come on, Ei - leen.

Bass Fig. 1

End Bass Fig. 1

Verse

w/ Bass Fig. 1 (3 3/4 times)

C   Em   F
1. Poor old John - nie Ray | sound - ed |sad up - on the ra - di - o; moved a |

C   G   C   Em
mil - lion hearts in mon - o. | Our moth - ers |cried, |

F   C   G   C
sang a - long; who'd blame them? | |You're grown. |

Em   F   C   G
So grown. Now | I must say more than e - ver: | Come on, Ei - leen. |

C   Em   F
Too, ra, loo, ra, | too, ra, loo, rye, | aye. And we can |

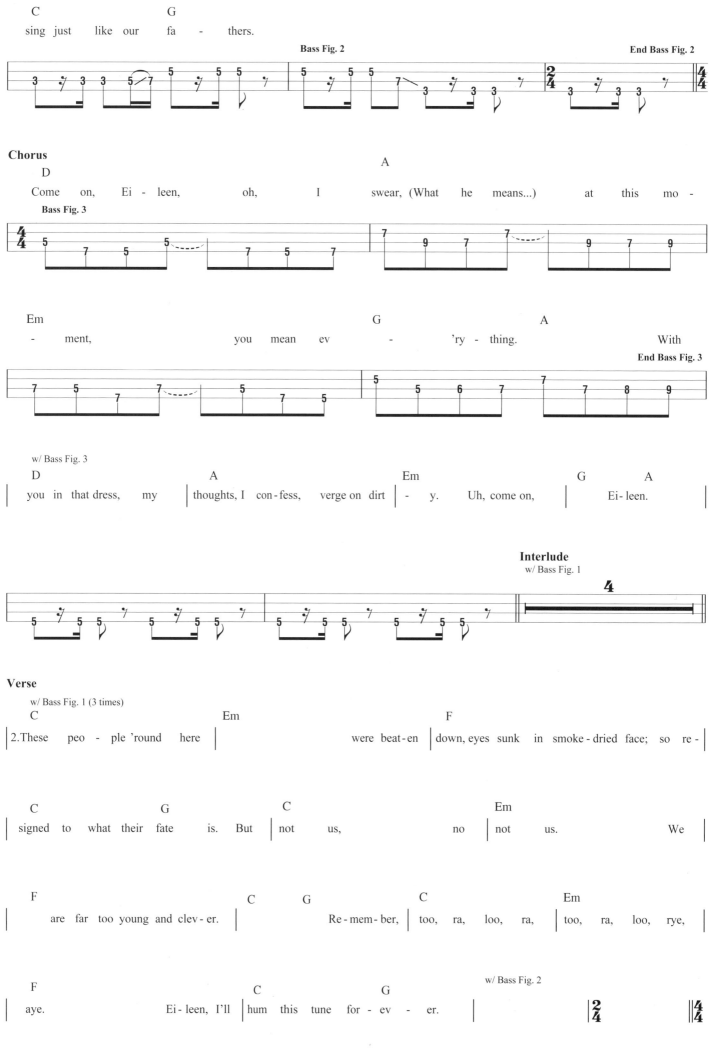

Chorus

w/ Bass Fig. 3 (2 3/4 times)

D   A   Em

Come on Ei - leen,   oh,   I | swear,   uh, come on, | let's   take off ev -

G   A   D   A

- 'ry - thing. That | pret - ty red dress, Ei - | leen,   uh, come on, |

Em   G   A

let's,   uh, come on, | Ei - leen.   That |

D   A   Em

pret - ty red dress, Ei - | leen,   uh, come on, | let's,   uh, come on, |

Moderately

G   A   D

Ei - leen.   Please.

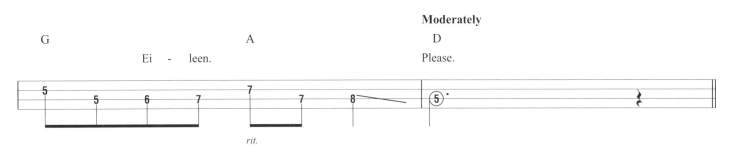

rit.

Bridge

D   F#m

Come on,   Ei - leen. Too, loo, rye, aye. Come on,   Ei - leen. Too, loo, rye,

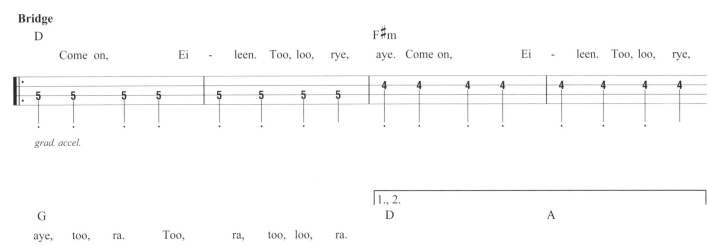

grad. accel.

                                     1., 2.

G   D   A

aye, too, ra.   Too,   ra, too, loo, ra.

3.

Outro-Chorus
Moderately

Repeat and fade

w/ Bass Fig. 3

D   A

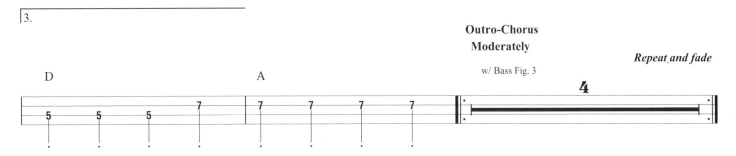

Counting Stars

Words and Music by Ryan Tedder

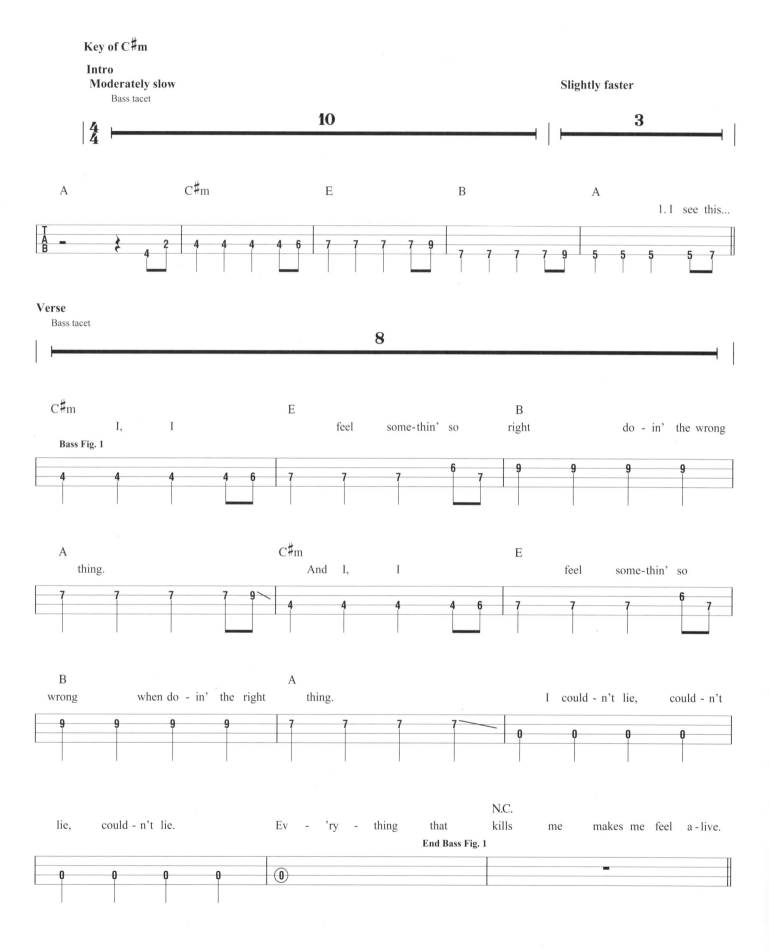

% Chorus

C#m ... E
Late - ly I been, I been los - in' sleep

Bass Fig. 2

B ... A ... C#m
dream - in' a - bout the things that we could be. But, ba - by, I been,

E ... B ... A
I been pray - in' hard. Said no more count - in' dol-lars, we'll be count - in' stars.

End Bass Fig. 2

w/ Bass Fig. 2

C#m ... E ... B
Late - ly I been, I been los - in' sleep dream - in' a - bout the things that

A ... C#m ... E
we could be. But, ba - by, I been, I been pray - in' hard.

To Coda 1 ⊕
To Coda 2 ⊕

B ... A
Said no more count - in' dol - lars, we'll be, we'll be count - in'

Interlude

C#m ... E ... B ... A
stars. 2. I feel your...

Verse

Bass tacet

4

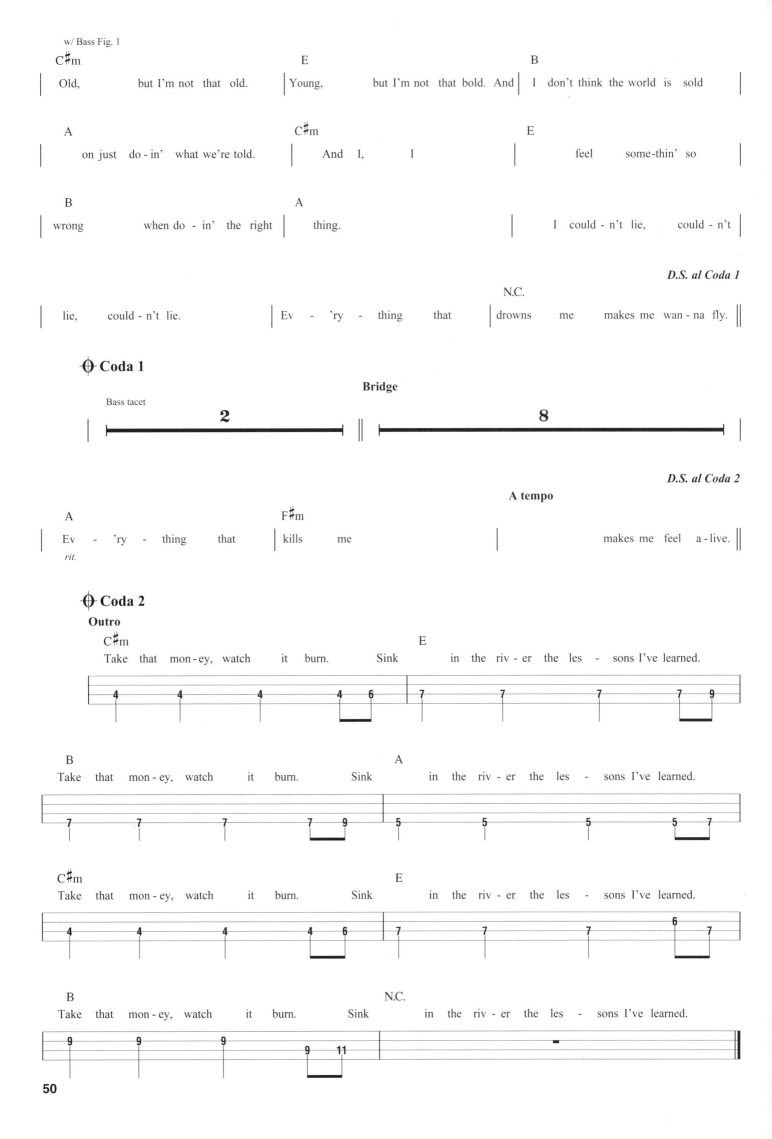

Dance Monkey

Words and Music by Toni Watson

5-string bass:
(low to high) B-E-A-D-G

Key of F♯m

Intro

Moderately

Bass tacet

F♯m   D   E

4/4

Verse

C♯m   F♯m   D

1. They say, "Oh, my God, I see the way you shine. Take your hand,

E   C♯m

my dear, and place them both in mine." You know you

F♯m   D

stopped me dead while I was pass - ing by. And now I beg

E   C♯m

to see you dance just one more time. Ooh, I

Pre-Chorus

F♯m   D

see you, see you, see you ev - 'ry time, and oh, my, I,

E   C♯m

I, I, I like your style. You, you

F♯m   D

make me, make me, make me want to cry, and now I beg

E   N.C.

to see you dance just one more time. So they say:

Chorus

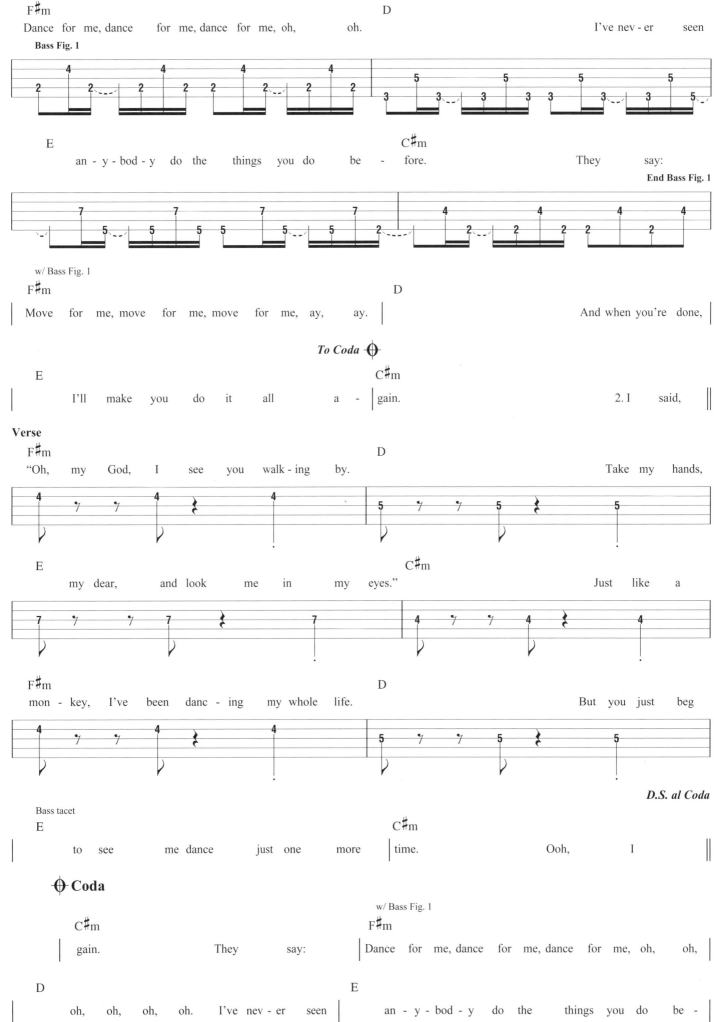

F#m   D

Dance for me, dance for me, dance for me, oh,   oh.   I've nev - er seen

Bass Fig. 1

E   C#m

an - y - bod - y do the things you do be - fore.   They say:

End Bass Fig. 1

w/ Bass Fig. 1

F#m   D

Move for me, move for me, move for me, ay,   ay.   And when you're done,

To Coda ⊕

E   C#m

I'll make you do it all a - gain.   2. I said,

Verse

F#m   D

"Oh, my God, I see you walk - ing by.   Take my hands,

E   C#m

my dear, and look me in my eyes."   Just like a

F#m   D

mon - key, I've been danc - ing my whole life.   But you just beg

D.S. al Coda

Bass tacet

E   C#m

to see me dance just one more time.   Ooh, I

⊕ **Coda**

w/ Bass Fig. 1

C#m   F#m

gain.   They say: Dance for me, dance for me, dance for me, oh,   oh,

D   E

oh, oh, oh, oh. I've nev - er seen   an - y - bod - y do the things you do be -

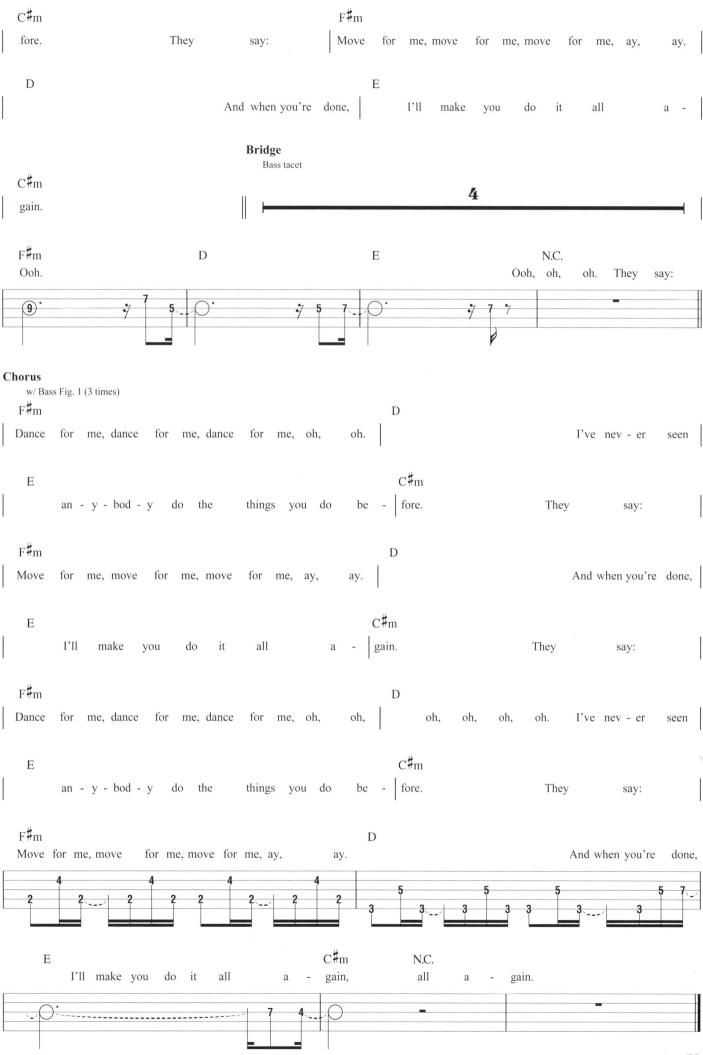

C#m   **F#m**
fore.   They   say: Move   for   me,   move   for   me, move   for   me,   ay,   ay.

D   **E**
And when you're done,   I'll   make   you   do   it   all   a -

Bridge
Bass tacet

C#m
gain.

F#m   **D**   **E**   **N.C.**
Ooh.   Ooh, oh,   oh.   They   say:

Chorus
w/ Bass Fig. 1 (3 times)

F#m   **D**
Dance   for   me,   dance   for   me,   dance   for   me,   oh,   oh.   I've   nev - er   seen

E   **C#m**
     an - y - bod - y   do   the   things   you   do   be - fore.   They   say:

F#m   **D**
Move   for   me,   move   for   me,   move   for   me,   ay,   ay.   And when you're done,

E   **C#m**
     I'll   make   you   do   it   all   a - gain.   They   say:

F#m   **D**
Dance   for   me,   dance   for   me,   dance   for   me,   oh,   oh,   oh,   oh,   oh,   oh.   I've   nev - er   seen

E   **C#m**
     an - y - bod - y   do   the   things   you   do   be - fore.   They   say:

F#m   **D**
Move   for   me,   move   for   me,   move   for   me,   ay,   ay.   And when you're   done,

E   **C#m**   **N.C.**
     I'll   make   you   do   it   all   a - gain,   all   a - gain.

Crazy Little Thing Called Love

Words and Music by Freddie Mercury

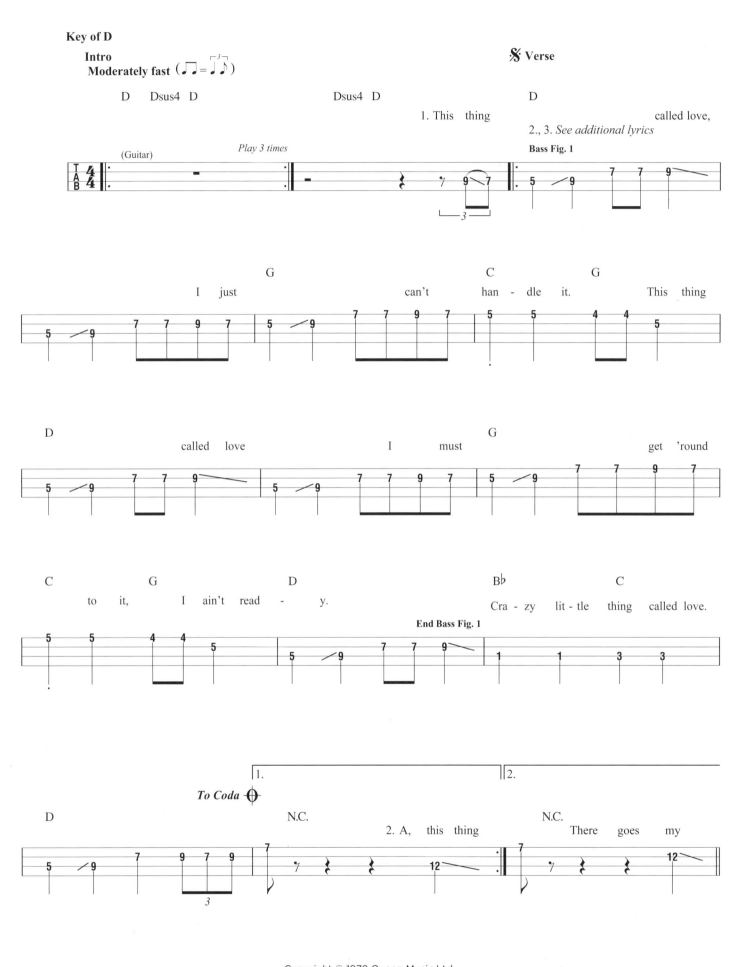

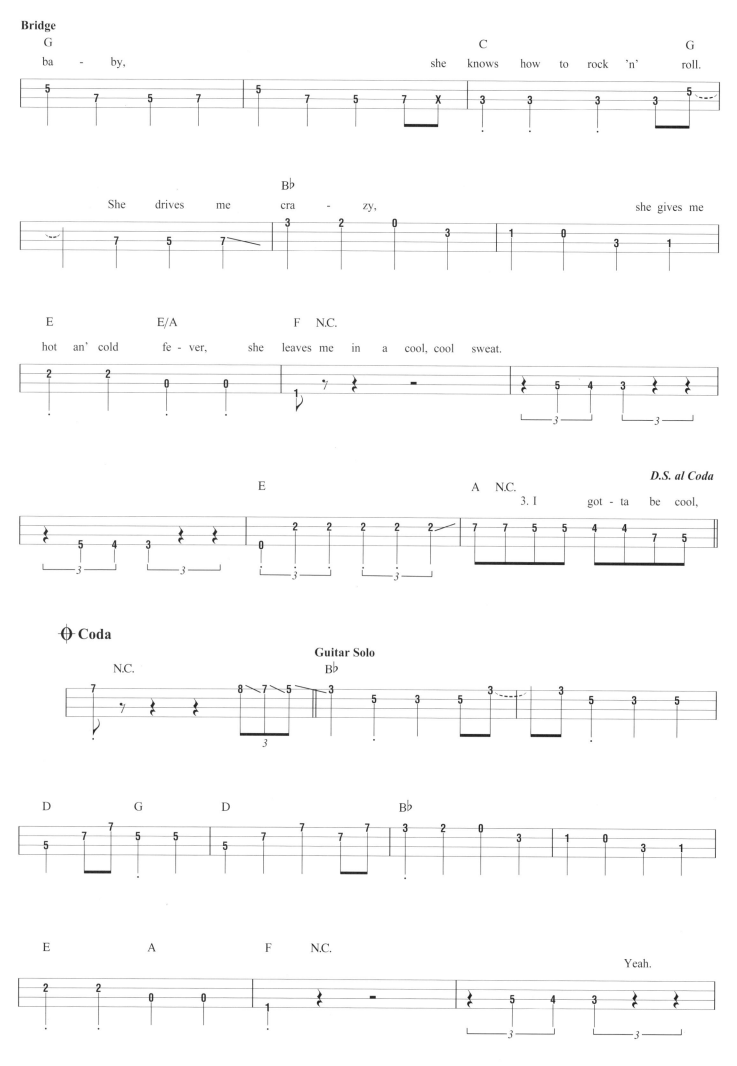

56

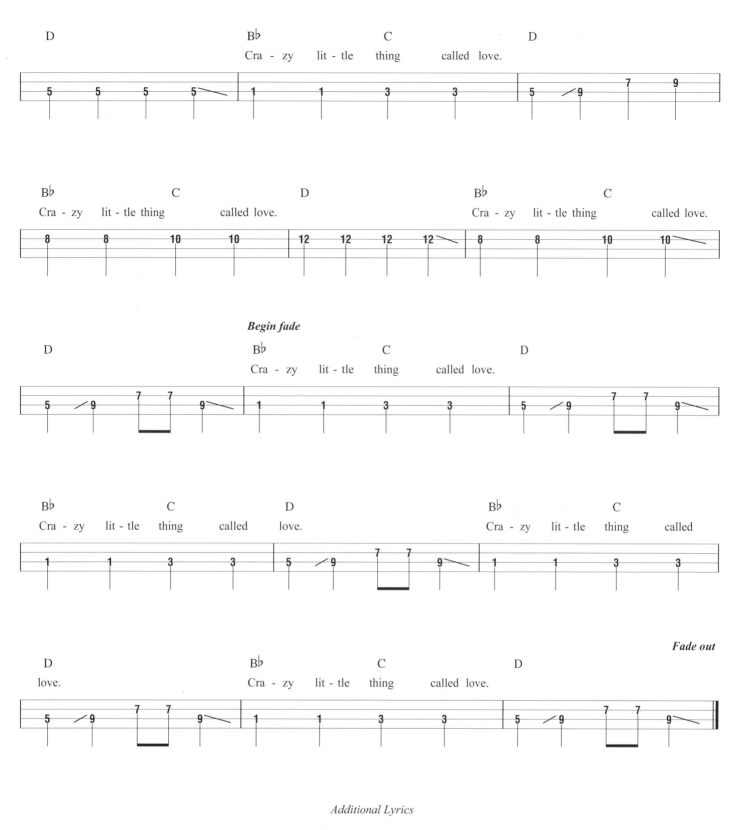

Additional Lyrics

2. A, this thing called love,
   It cries in a cradle all night.
   It swings, it jives,
   Shakes all over like a jellyfish.
   I kinda like it.
   Crazy little thing called love.

3. I've gotta be cool, relax,
   Get hip, get on my tracks.
   Take a back seat, hitchhike,
   Take a long ride on my motorbike
   Until I'm ready.
   Crazy little thing called love.

Don't Start Now

Words and Music by Dua Lipa, Caroline Ailin, Ian Kirkpatrick and Emily Schwartz

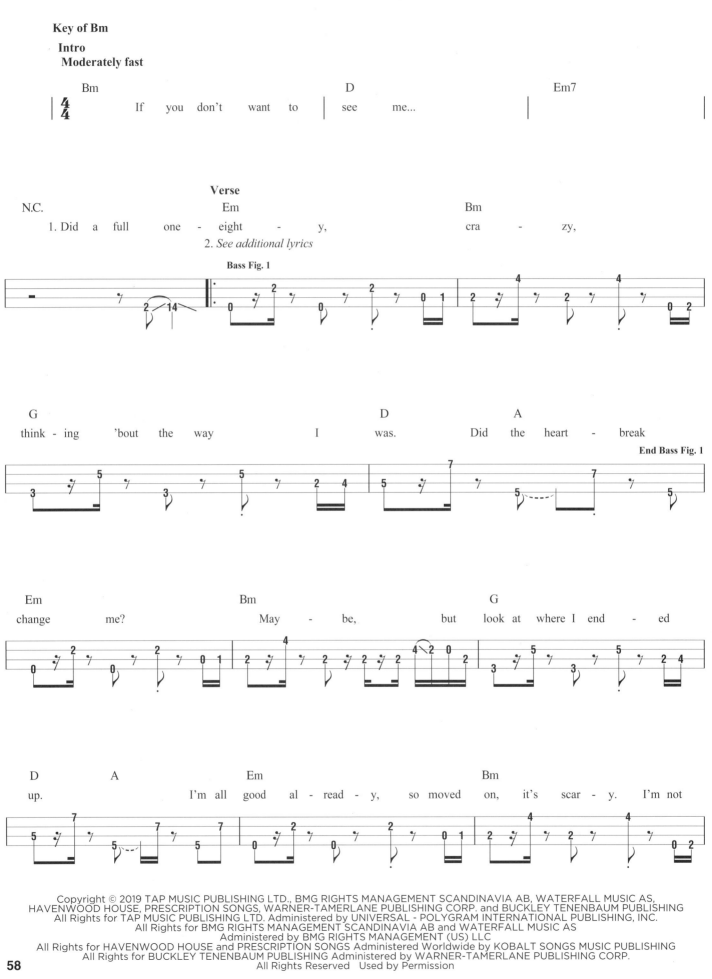

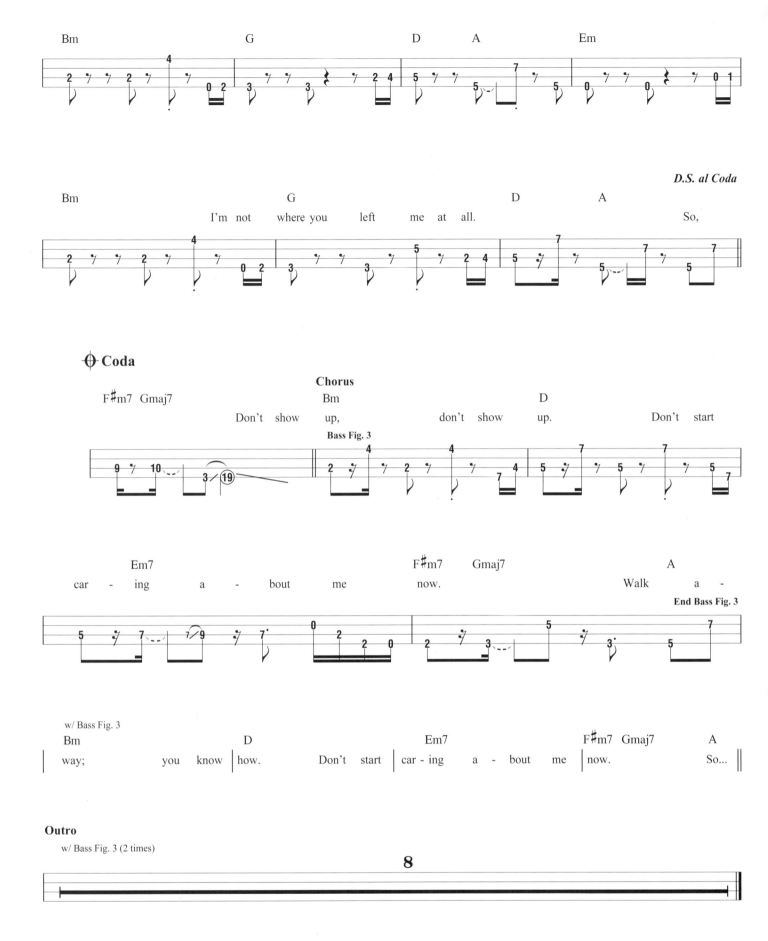

Outro

w/ Bass Fig. 3 (2 times)

Additional Lyrics

2. Aren't you the guy who tried to
Hurt me with the word "goodbye"?
Though it took some time to survive you,
I'm better on the other side.
I'm all good already, so moved on it's scary.
I'm not where you left me at all.

Don't You
(Forget About Me)

from the Universal Picture THE BREAKFAST CLUB
Words and Music by Keith Forsey and Steve Schiff

Key of Em

Intro
Moderate Rock

Hey, hey, hey, hey.   Oo.

Verse

E5   D

1. Won't you come see a - bout me?
2. *See additional lyrics*

Bass Fig. 1

A   D

I'll be a - lone,   danc - ing, you know it, ba - by.

End Bass Fig. 1

w/ Bass Fig. 1 (3 times)

E5   D   A

Tell me your | trou - bles and doubts; | giv - ing me ev - 'ry - thing |

D   E5   D

in - side and out. And | love's strange; so | real in the dark. |

A   D   E5

Think of the ten - der things | that we were work - ing on. | Slow change may |

D   A   D

pull us a - part. | When the light gets in | - to your heart, ba - by, ‖

Chorus
w/ Bass Fig. 1 (1 1/2 times)

E5   D   A

don't you | for - get a - bout me. |

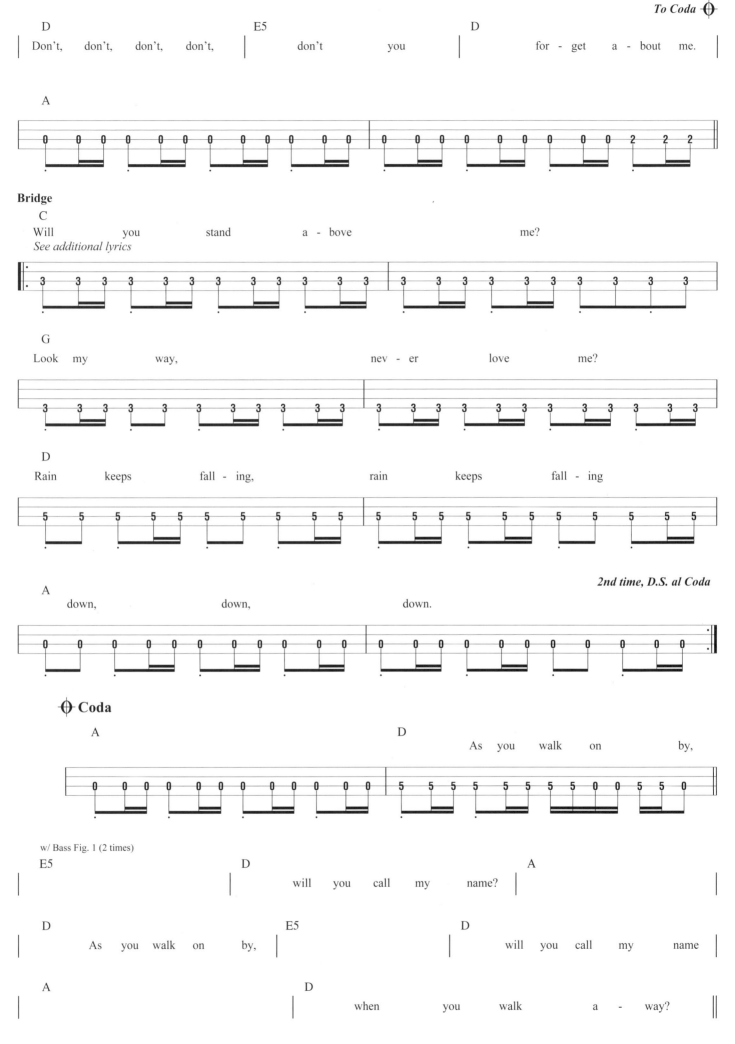

Interlude

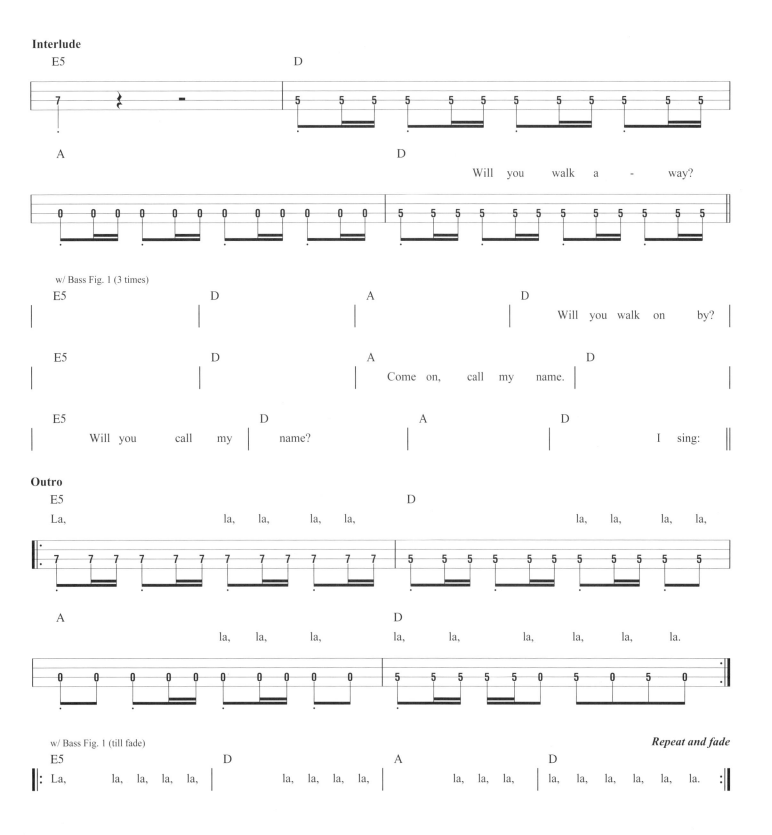

w/ Bass Fig. 1 (3 times)

Will you walk on by?

Come on, call my name.

Will you call my name? I sing:

Outro

La, la, la, la, la, la, la, la, la,

la, la, la, la, la, la, la, la, la.

w/ Bass Fig. 1 (till fade)

Repeat and fade

La, la, la, la, la, la, la, la, la, la, la, la, la, la, la, la.

Additional Lyrics

Bridge Will you recognize me,
Call my name or walk on by?
Rain keeps falling, rain keeps falling
Down, down, down, down.

2. Don't you try and pretend.
It's my feeling we'll win in the end.
I won't harm you or touch your defenses;
Vanity and security.
Don't you forget about me.
I'll be alone, dancing, you know it, baby.
Going to take you apart;
I'll put us back together at heart, baby.

Don't You Want Me

Words and Music by Phil Oakey, Adrian Wright and Jo Callis

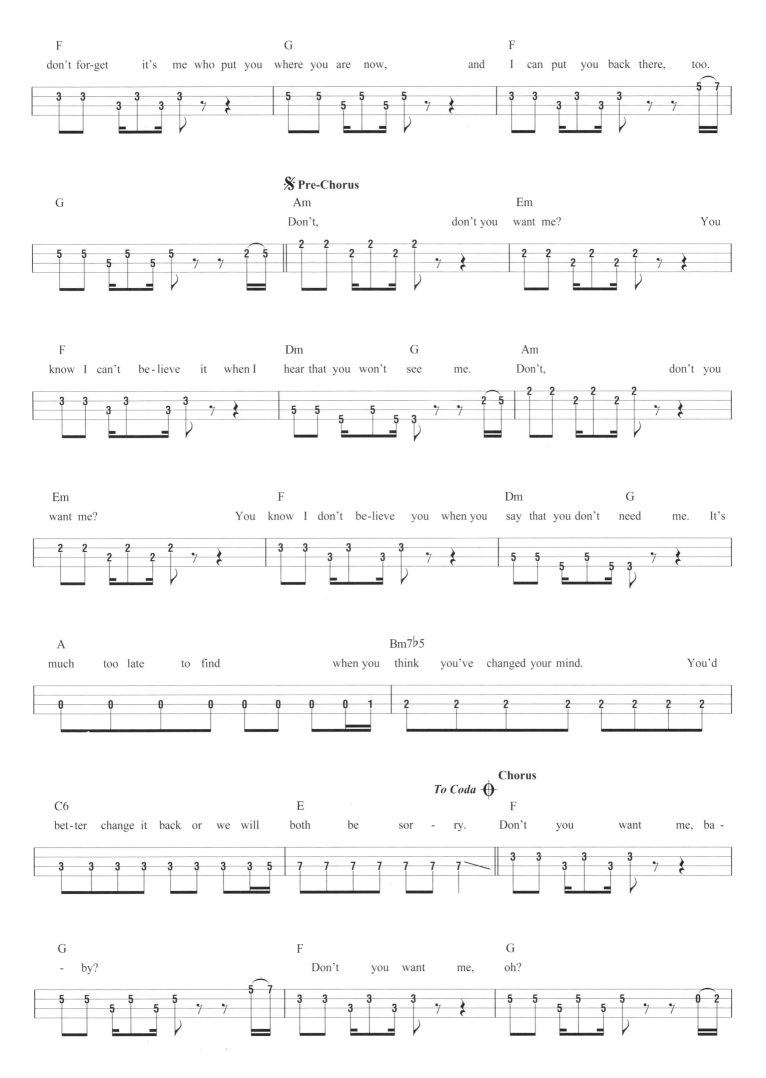

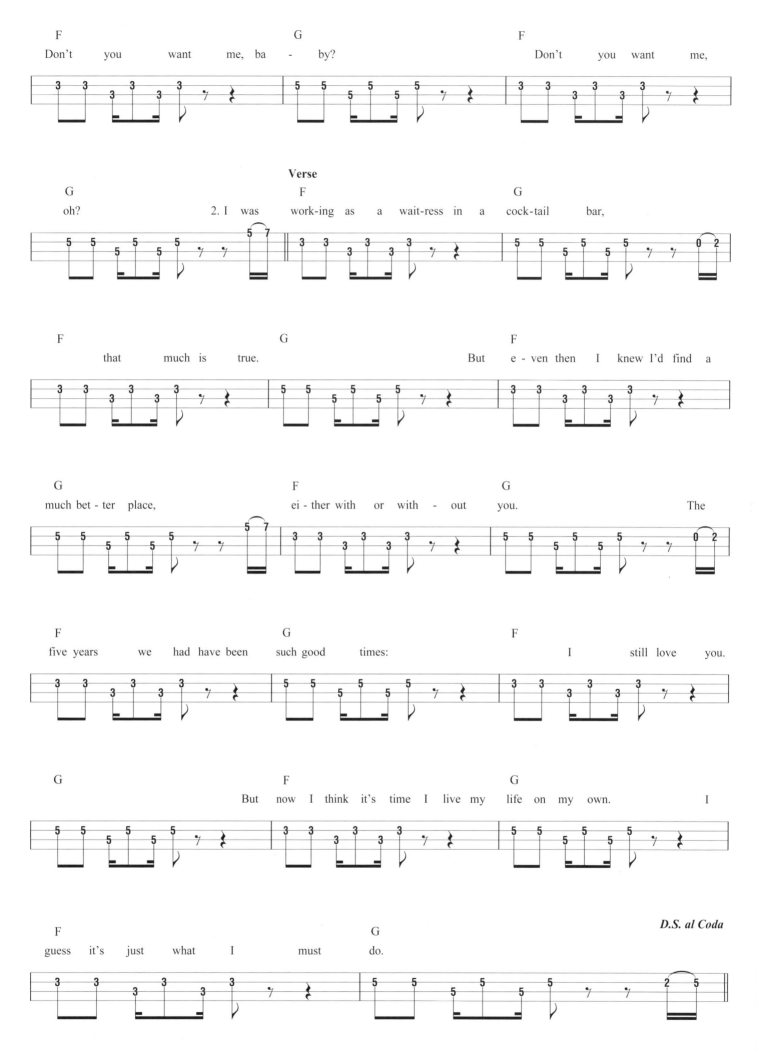

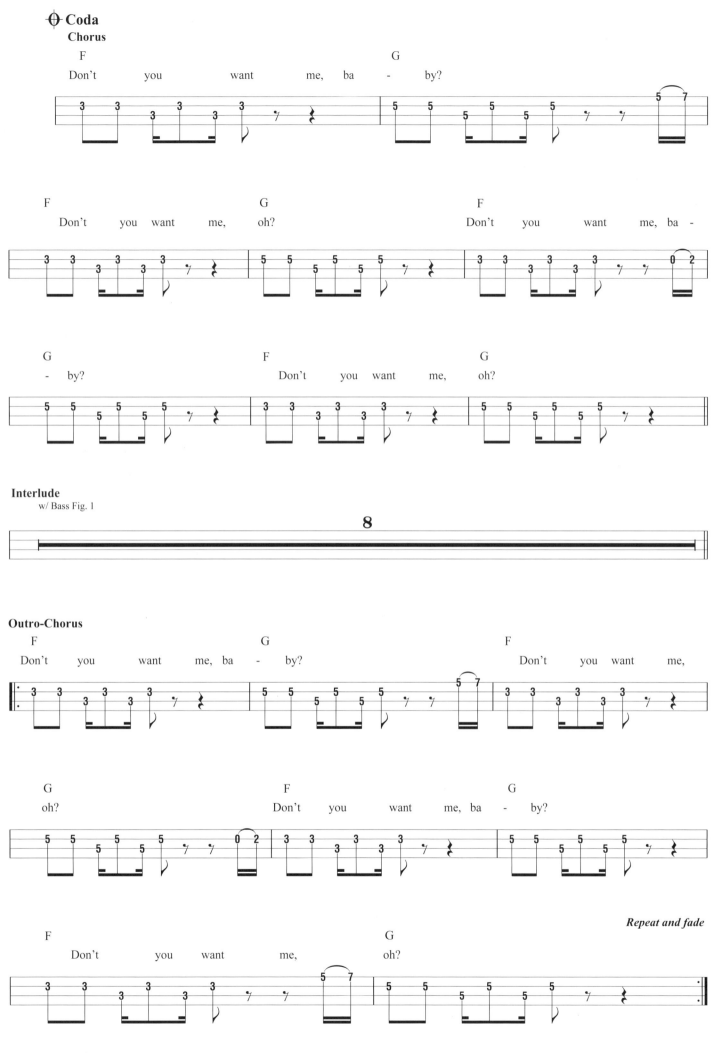

Every Little Thing She Does Is Magic

Music and Lyrics by Sting

Key of D

Intro
Moderately fast

G | A | G/B | A/C# | A/C#

Bass Fig. 1 ... *End Bass Fig. 1*

1.Though I've

(TAB intro: 3 ... 5 ... 2 | 4 | 4)

%\ Verse
w/ Bass Fig. 1 (3 times)

G		A		G/B

tried be - fore to tell her of the feel - ings I have for her
2. See additional lyrics

| A/C# | | G | | A |

in my heart,

| G/B | A/C# | | G |

ev - 'ry time that I come near

To Coda ⊕

| A | | G/B | | A/C# |

her, I just lose my nerve as I've done from the start.

D G A D A D A D

Ev - 'ry lit - tle

(TAB: 5 · 5 7 7 5 7 7 5 7 7 5 · 7 5 7 5 0 ·)
steady gliss.

Chorus

| A | | D | | A |

thing she does is mag - ic. Ev - 'ry - thing she do just turns me on.

(TAB: 5 · 4 7 5 5 4 4 7 5 · 4)

| D | | A | | D |

E - ven though my life be - fore was trag - ic, now I know my

(TAB: 5 5 4 7 5 5 · 4 7 5 5 5 4 7)

| A | | Bb | | C/F |

love for her goes on.

(TAB: 5 · 4 ① ③)

G   A   G/B   A/C#

2. Do   I

⊕ Coda

D G A D   A   D   A   D N.C.

Ev-'ry lit-tle

Chorus

A   D   A

thing she does is mag - ic.   Ev-'ry-thing she do just turns me on.

D   A   D

E - ven though my life be - fore was trag - ic,   now I know my

A   Bb   C/F   Bb   C/F

love for her goes on.

Bridge

Bb   Am7   Gm7   Am7

I re-solved to call her up   a thou-sand times a day,

Gm7   Am7   Bb

and ask her if she'll mar - ry me   in some old - fash-ioned way,

Am7   Bb   C

but my si - lent fears have gripped me   long be - fore

Bb   C   Bb   C

I reached the phone,   long be - fore my tongue has tripped me.   Must I

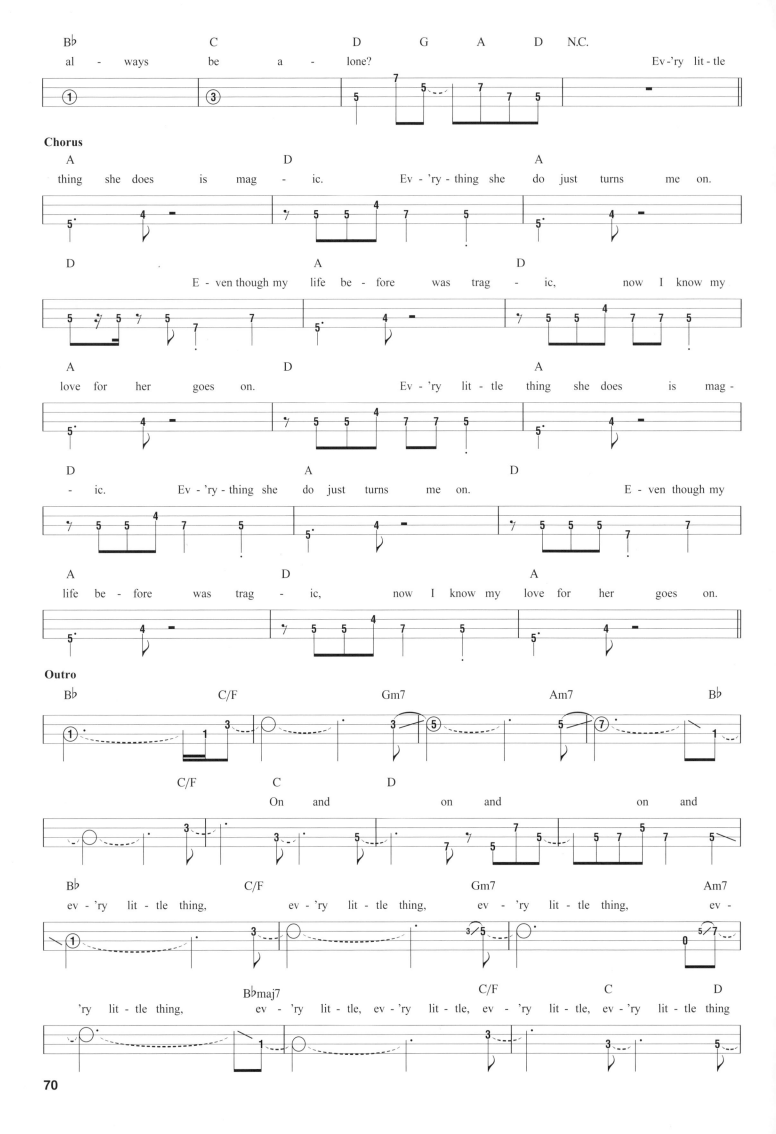

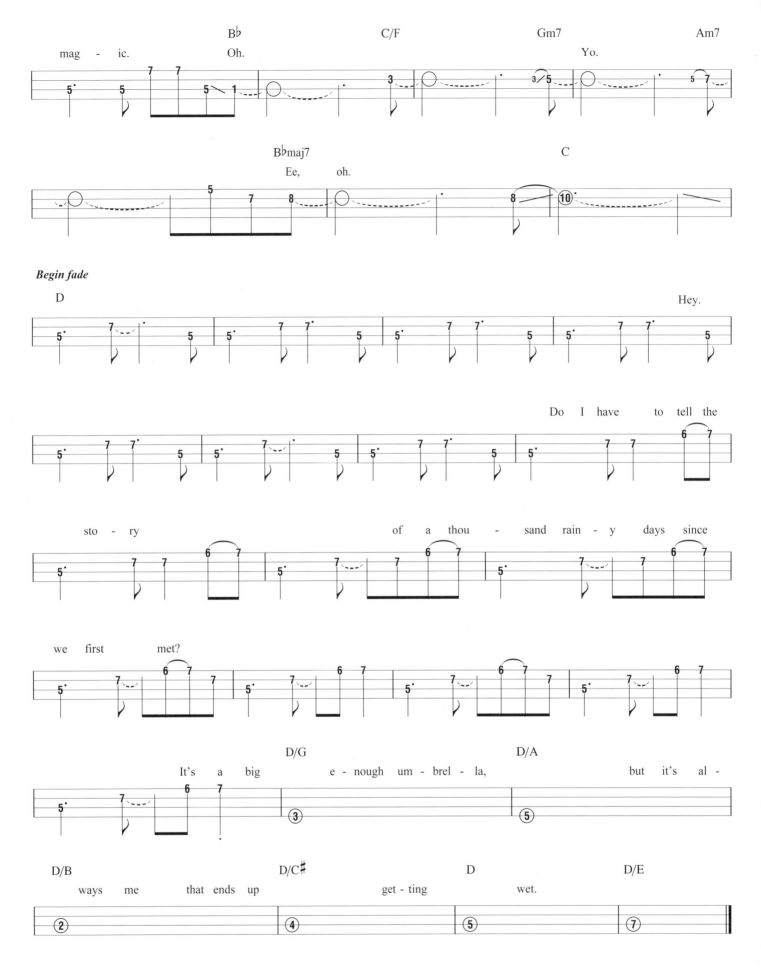

Additional Lyrics

2. Do I have to tell the story
   Of a thousand rainy days since we first met?
   It's a big enough umbrella,
   But it's always me who ends up getting wet.

Everybody Wants to Rule the World

Words and Music by Ian Stanley, Roland Orzabal and Christopher Hughes

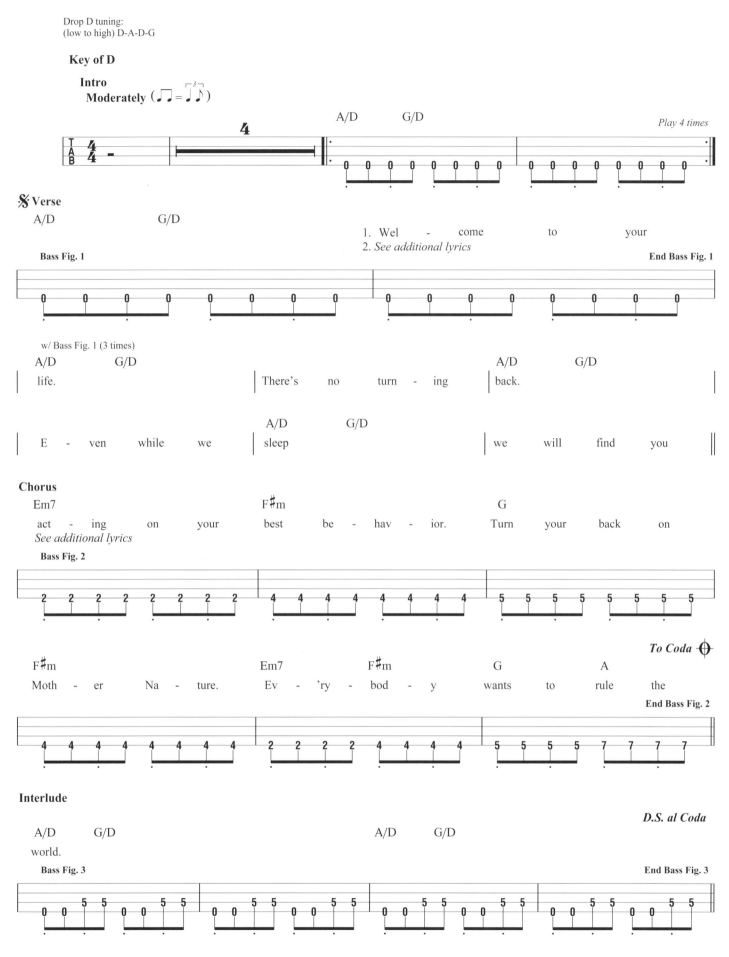

Guitar Solo

w/ Bass Fig. 3 (2 times)

A

8

Chorus

w/ Bass Fig. 2 (2 times)

Em7	F#m	G	F#m
I can't stand that	in - de - ci - sion,	mar - ried with a	lack of vis - ion.

Em7	F#m	G	A
Ev - 'ry - bod - y	wants to rule the world.		

Em7		F#m	
Say that you'll	nev - er, nev - er, nev - er, nev - er need it.		

G	F#m	Em7 F#m	G A
One head - line;	why be - lieve it?	Ev - 'ry - bod - y	wants to rule the

Guitar Solo

G	D	A	G	D	A
world.					

Chorus

w/ Bass Fig. 2

Em7	F#m	G
All for free - dom	and for pleas - ure.	Noth - ing ev - er

F#m	Em7 F#m	G A
lasts for - ev - er.	Ev - 'ry - bod - y	wants to rule the

Outro-Guitar Solo

w/ Bass Fig. 3 (till fade)

Repeat and fade

A/D G/D		A/D G/D	
world.			

Additional Lyrics

2. It's my own design. It's my own remorse.
Help me to decide. Help me make the

Chorus Most of freedom and of pleasure.
Nothing ever lasts forever.
Ev'rybody wants to rule the world.

Feels

Words and Music by Calvin Harris, Pharrell Williams, Wayne Vaughn,
Maurice White, Brittany Hazzard, Sean Anderson and Katy Perry

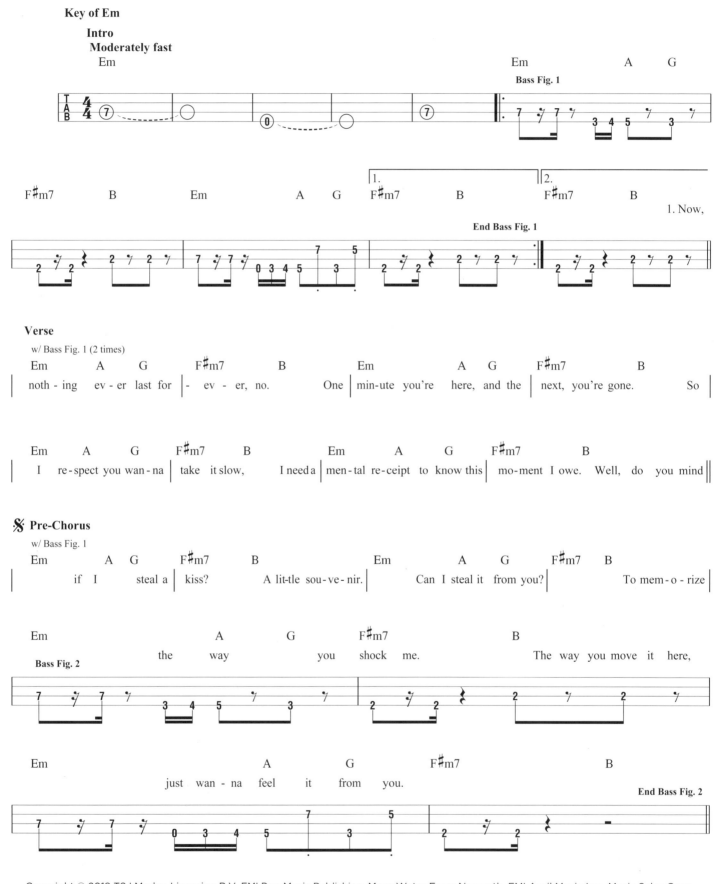

Chorus

1st time, w/ Bass Fig. 1 (2 times)
2nd time, w/ Bass Fig. 1 (1 3/4 times)

Em			A	G	F#m7		B		Em		A	G

Don't be a-fraid to catch feels, ride drop-top and chase thrills.

F#m7		B		Em			A	G	F#m7		B	

I know you ain't a-fraid to pop pills. Ba-by,

To Coda ⊕

Em			A	G	F#m7			B	

I know you ain't scared to catch feels, feels with me.

Verse

w/ Bass Fig. 1

Em			A	G	F#m7		B		Em		A	G

2. I'm your win-dow shop-per, suck-er for your love, oh. I'm wear-ing your gog-gles,

w/ Bass Fig. 2

F#m7		B		Em		A	G	F#m7		B	

vir-tu-al re-al-i-ty. It ain't what it cost ya; it might be a dol-lar.

D.S. al Coda

Em			A	G	F#m7			B	

As long as it shocks ya, mem-o-ry, e-lec-tric-i-ty. Well, do you mind

⊕ Coda

Bridge

F#m7		B		Em	

feels with me. God-damn, I know you love to make an en-trance.
See additional lyrics

Do you like get-ting paid or get-ting paid at-ten-tion? You mixed the wrong guys with the right in-ten-tions.

In the same bed, but it still feel long dis-tance. You're look-ing for a lit-tle more con-sis-ten-cy, but when you

stop look-ing, you gon' find what's meant to be. And hon-est-ly, I'm way too done with the hoes. I

Am　　　　　　**Bm**

1.
cut off all my ex - es for your X and O's. I wear your fave co - logne just to get you a - lone.

C　　　　　　**D**　**C/E**　　　**C**　　　　**D**　**N.C.**

2.

Chorus
1st time, w/ Bass Fig. 1 (2 times)
2nd time, w/ Bass Fig. 1

Em　　　　　　　　　　　　　　　**A**　　**G**　**F#m7**　　　　　**B**

Don't be a - fraid to catch feels,

2nd time, w/ Bass Fig. 2

Em　　　　**A**　**G**　**F#m7**　　　**B**　　　　**Em**　　　　**A**　**G**

ride drop - top and chase thrills. I know you ain't a - fraid to pop pills.

F#m7　　　　**B**　　　　　　**Em**　　　　　　**A**　**G**

Ba - by, I know you ain't scared to catch feels,

1.
F#m7　　　　　**B**

feels with me.

2.
F#m7　　　　　**B**

feels with me.

Additional Lyrics

Bridge　I feel my old flings was just preparing me.
　　　　When I say I want you, say it back, parakeet.
　　　　Fly you first-class through the air, Air B'n'B.
　　　　I'm the best you had; you just be comparing me to me.
　　　　I'm a @ this at you; if I put you on my phone
　　　　And upload it, it'd get maximum views.
　　　　I came through in the clutch with the lipsticks and phones.
　　　　Wear your fave cologne just to get you alone.

Fireball

Words and Music by Armando Christian Perez, Eric Frederic, Ilsey Juber, Andreas Schuller, Tom Peyton, John Ryan and Joseph Spargur

Key of F

Intro
Moderate Latin
Bass tacet

F   E♭   F   E♭

Ba - by, ba - by, ba - by, ba - by, ba - by, ba - by, ba - by, ba - by, ba - by, I'm on fire. I tell her

Bass Fig. 1

F   E♭   F   N.C.

ba - by, ba - by, ba - by, ba - by, ba - by, ba - by, ba - by, ba - by, ba - by, I'm a fire - ball.

End Bass Fig. 1

Chorus

F   E♭   F   E♭   F   E♭   F   E♭

Woo, woo!   Woo, woo!

Bass Fig. 2

F   E♭   F   E♭   F   E♭   F   N.C.

Woo, woo!   Fire - ball. 1. I

End Bass Fig. 2

Verse

F   E♭   F   E♭

saw, I came, I con - quered or should I say I saw, I con - quered, I came? They say the

Bass Fig. 3

F   E♭   F   N.C.

chi - co on fire, he ain't no liar, while y'all slip - pin' he run - nin' the game. Now

End Bass Fig. 3

F · · · Eb · · · F · · · Eb

big bang boog-ie get that kit-ty lit-tle noog-ie in a nice, nice lit-tle shade. I gave

F · · · Eb · · · F · · · N.C.

Su-zie lit-tle pat up on the boot-y and she turned a-round and said, "Walk this way." I was born

𝄋 Pre-Chorus

2nd time, bass tacet, next 8 meas.

F · · · Eb · · · F · · · Eb

in a flame. Ma-ma said

Bass Fig. 4 · · · · · · · · · · **End Bass Fig. 4**

w/ Bass Fig. 4 (3 times)

F · Eb · · F · Eb · · F · Eb

that ev-ry-one would know my name. I'm the best you've ev-er had.

F · Eb · · F · Eb · · F · Eb

If you think I'm burn-ing out, I nev-er am. I'm on

1st time, bass tacet
2nd time, w/ Bass Fig. 4 (3 times)

F · Eb · F · Eb · N.C.

Play 3 times

𝄆 fire. | I'm on 𝄇 fire. | Fire - ball. 𝄇

Chorus

1st time, w/ Bass Fig. 2
2nd time, w/ Bass Fig. 2 (1st meas., 8 times)

F · Eb · F Eb · F · Eb · F Eb

Woo, | woo! | Woo, | woo!

To Coda ⊕

F · Eb · F Eb · F · Eb · F N.C.

Woo, | woo! | Fire - ball. 𝄇

Verse

w/ Bass Fig. 3 (2 times)

F · · · Eb · · · F · · · Eb

2. Sticks and stones may break my bones but | I don't care what y'all say. 'Cause

F · · · Eb · · · F · · · N.C.

as the world turns, y'all boys gon' learn that this | chi-co right here don't play. That |

| F | E♭ | F | E♭ |

boy's from the bot - tom, bot - tom of the map; | M I A, U. S. A. | I gave

D.S. al Coda

| F | E♭ | F N.C. |

Su - zie lit - tle pat up on the boot - y and she turned a - round and | said, "Walk this way." | I was born ‖

⊕ **Coda**

| F | E♭ | F | E♭ |

Woo, | woo! | We're ‖

Interlude

Bass tacet

| F | E♭ | F | E♭ |

‖: tak - ing it, we're tak - ing it, we're tak - ing it down. We're | tak - ing it, we're tak - ing it, we're tak - ing it down. We're |

| F | E♭ | F | E♭ |

tak - ing it, we're tak - ing it, we're tak - ing it down. We're | tak - ing it, we're tak - ing it, we're tak - ing it down. We're :‖

w/ Bass Fig. 4 (3 1/2 times)

| F | E♭ | F | E♭ |

‖: bring - ing it, we're bring - ing it, we're bring - ing it back. We're | bring - ing it, we're bring - ing it, we're bring - ing it back. We're |

1.

| F | E♭ | F | E♭ |

bring - ing it, we're bring - ing it, we're bring - ing it back. We're | bring - ing it, we're bring - ing it, we're bring - ing it back. We're:‖

2.

w/ Bass Fig. 1 (last meas.)

| F | E♭ | F N.C. |

bring - ing it, we're bring - ing it, we're bring - ing it back. | Fire - ball. ‖

Chorus

| F E♭ F E♭ | F E♭ F E♭ |

Woo, | woo! | Woo, | woo! |

| F E♭ F E♭ | F E♭ F E♭ |

Woo, | woo! | Woo, | woo! |

| F E♭ F E♭ | F E♭ F E♭ |

Woo, | woo! | Woo, | woo! I tell her |

| F | E♭ | F | E♭ |

ba - by, ba - by, ba - by, ba - by, ba - by, ba - by, ba - by, ba - by, | ba - by, huh, I'm on fire. I tell her |

| F | E♭ | F N.C. |

ba - by, ba - by, ba - by, ba - by, ba - by, ba - by, ba - by, ba - by, | ba - by, I'm a fire - ball. ‖

Footloose

Theme from the Paramount Motion Picture FOOTLOOSE
Words by Dean Pitchford
Music by Kenny Loggins

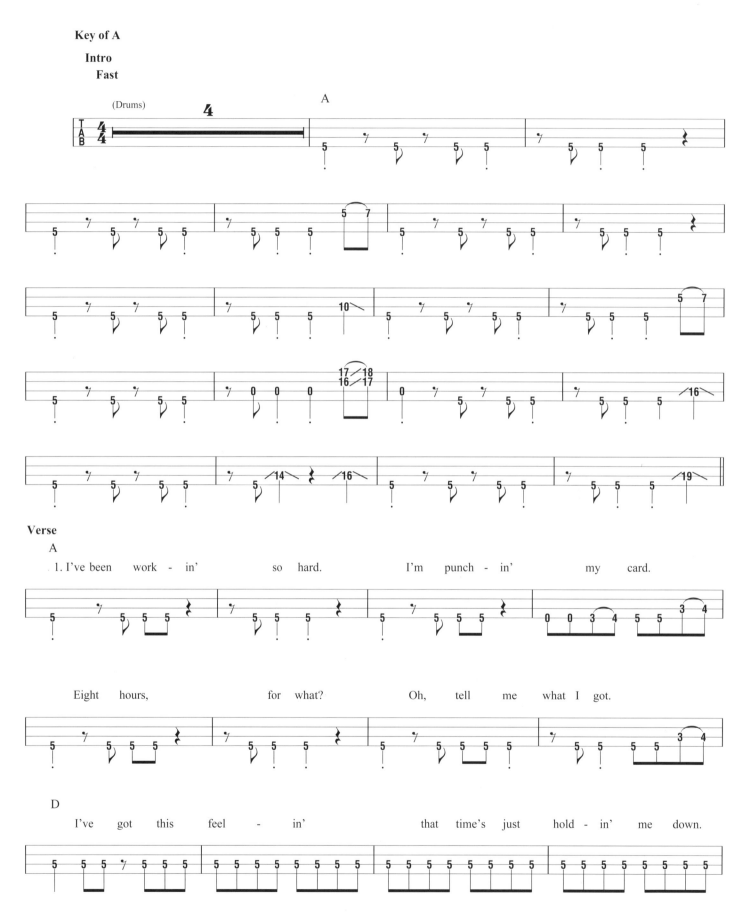

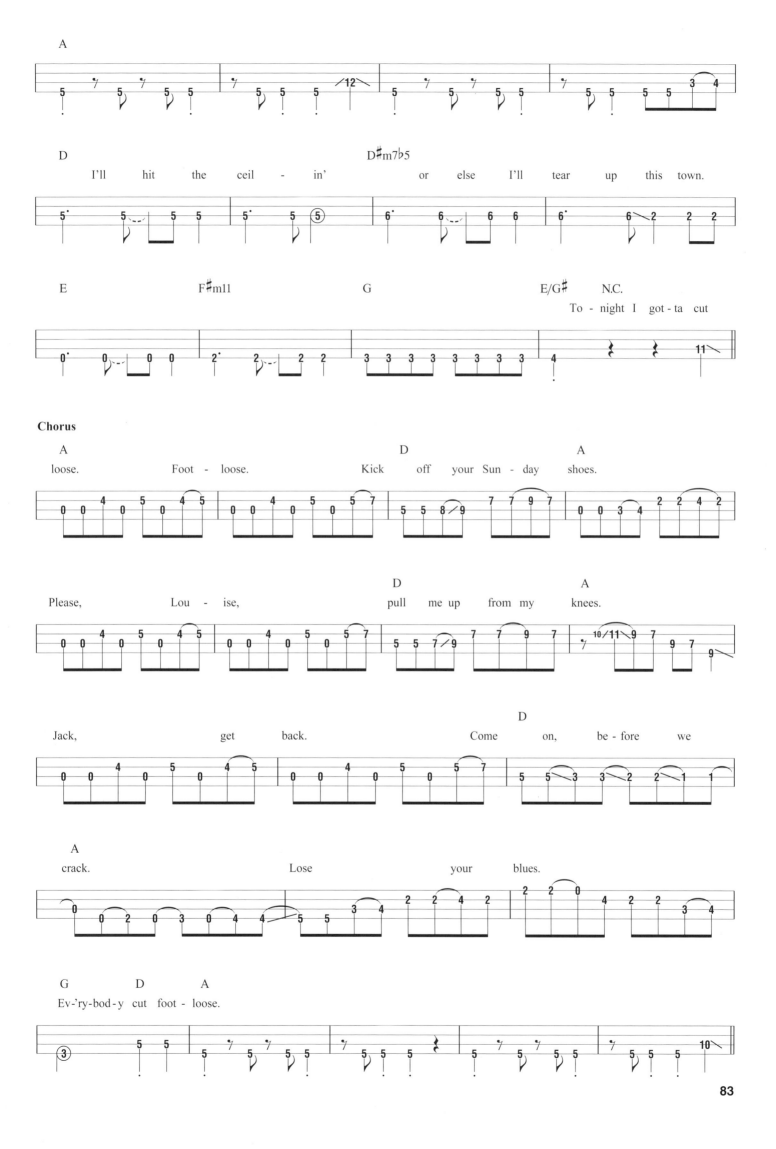

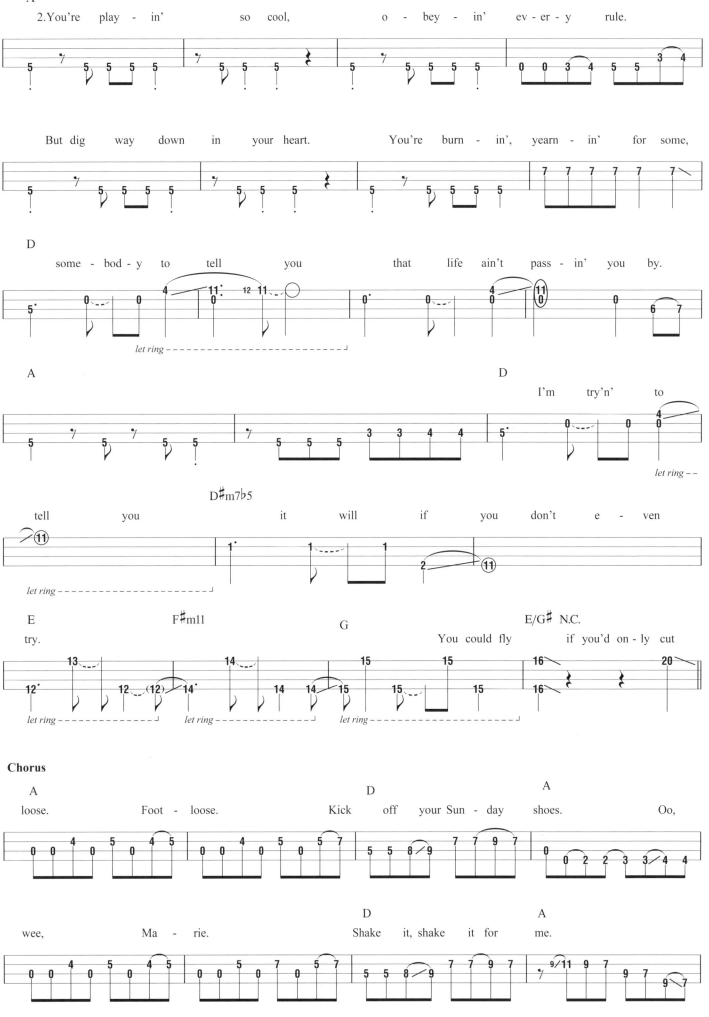

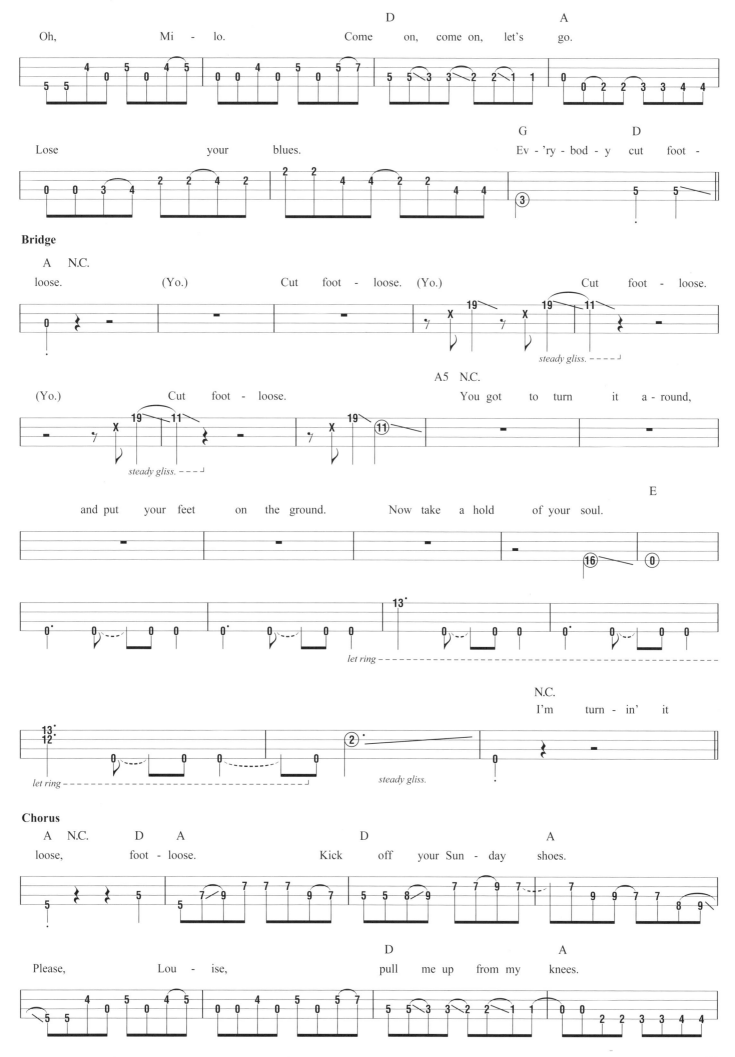

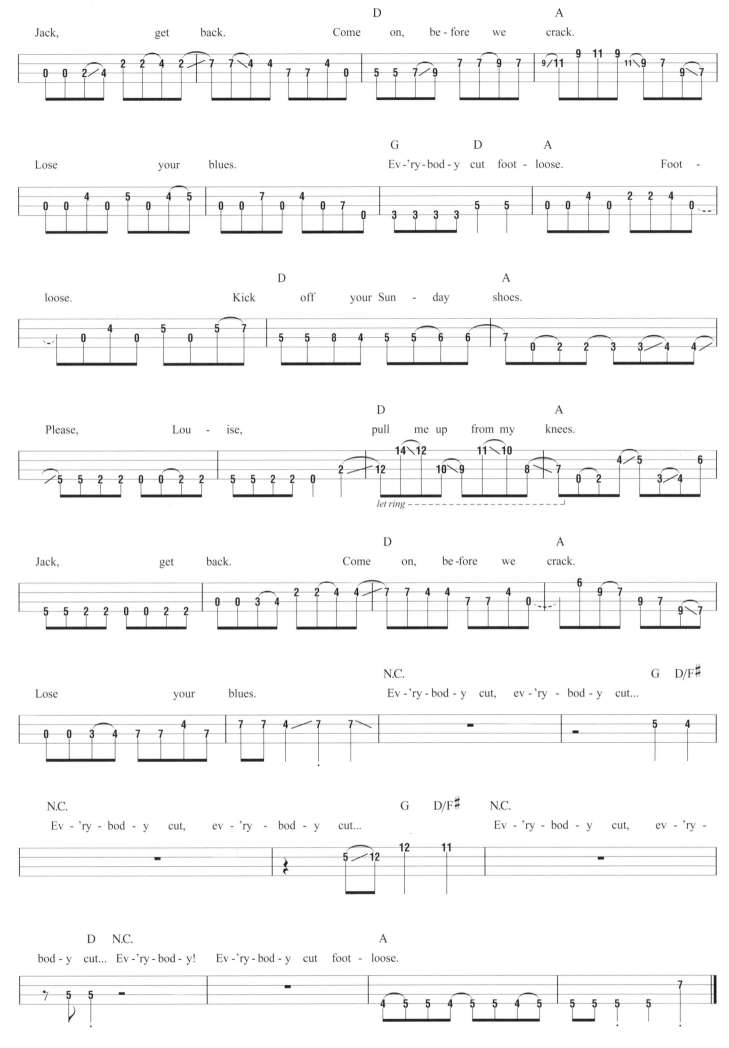

86

Havana

**Words and Music by Camila Cabello, Louis Bell, Pharrell Williams, Adam Feeney, Ali Tamposi,
Jeffery Lamar Williams, Brian Lee, Andrew Wotman, Brittany Hazzard and Kaan Gunesberk**

5-string bass:
(low to high) B-E-A-D-G

Key of Fm

Intro
Moderate Latin

Chorus

1. He

Verse

Gm		E♭ D7		Gm	E♭ D7	

did-n't walk up with that "How you do-ing?"   He said there's a lot of girls I can do with.   I'm

Bass Fig. 1   **End Bass Fig. 1**

w/ Bass Fig. 1

Gm   E♭ D7   Gm   E♭ D7

do-ing for-ev-er in a min-ute.   And Pa-pa says he got ma-lo in him.   He got me feel-ing like,

Pre-Chorus
Bass tacet

Gm   E♭ D7   Gm   E♭   D7

ooh.   I knew it when I   met him,   I loved him when I   left him.   Got me feel-ing like,

Gm   E♭ D7   Gm   E♭   D7 N.C.

ooh.   And then I had to   tell him   I had to go,   oh, na, na, na, na, na. Ha-

𝄋 Chorus
w/ Bass Fig. 1 (2 times)

Gm   E♭ D7   Gm   E♭   D7

van-a, ooh, na, na.   Half of my heart is in Ha- van-a, ooh, na, na.

Gm   E♭   D7

He took me back to East At- lan-ta, na, na, na.

To Coda ⊕

Gm   E♭   D7

Ah, but my heart is in Ha- van-a, my heart is in Ha- van-a, Ha-van-a, ooh, na...

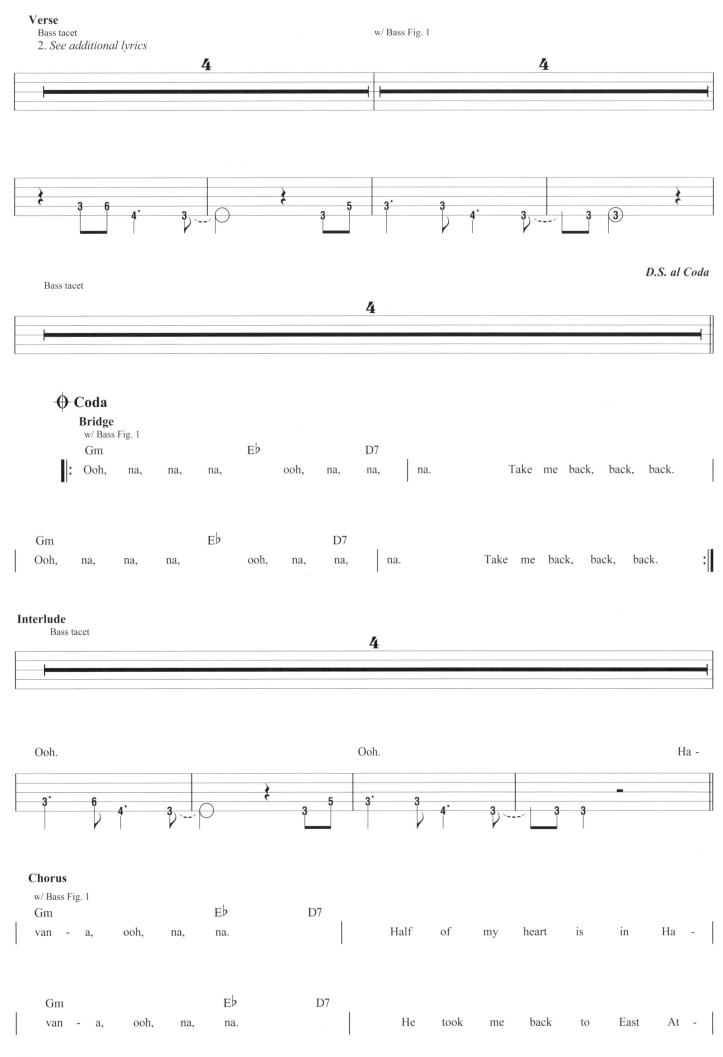

Outro

w/ Bass Fig. 1

Gm E♭ D7 Gm E♭ D7

na. Ooh, na, na, | na. Ooh, na, na, | na.

Gm E♭ D7 Gm E♭ D7

Ooh, na, na, na. Ooh, na, na,

N.C.

na. Ha - van - a, ooh, na, | na.

Additional Lyrics

2. Jeffery.
   Just graduated, fresh on campus, mmm.
   Fresh out East Atlanta with no manners, damn.
   Fresh out East Atlanta.
   Bump on her bumper like a traffic jam.
   Hey, I was quick to pay that girl like Uncle Sam.
   Back it on me, shawty cravin' on me.
   Get to diggin' on me.
   She waited on me.
   Shawty cakin' on me, got the bacon on me.
   This is history in the makin' on me.
   Point blank, close range, that be.
   If it cost a million, that's me.
   I was gettin' mula, man, they feel me.

Get Down On It

Words and Music by Ronald Bell, James Taylor, George Brown,
Robert Bell, Claydes Smith, Spike Mickens and Eumir Deodato

Key of Em

Intro
Moderately

Chorus

Verse

Em   Bm7   Am7/D

(Get your back   up   off   the wall.)   'Cause | I   heard   all   the   peo - ple say - in':

Verse

w/ Bass Fig. 1 (2 times)

Em   Bm7   Am7   Bm7

3. How ya gon - na do it if ya real - ly don't wan - na dance,   by stand - in' on the wall?

Em   Bm7   Am7/D

(Get your back   up   off   the wall.)   Tell me.

Em   Bm7   Am7   Bm7

How ya gon - na do it if ya real - ly won't take a chance,   by stand - in' on the wall?

Em   Bm7   Am7/D

(Get your back   up   off   the wall.)   'Cause | I   heard   all   the   peo - ple say - in':

Chorus

Em   Bm7   Am7   Bm7 Em   Bm7   Am7/D

Get down on it,   get down on it.   Get down on it,   get down on it.

Play 3 times

Interlude

Em   Am/D   Em   Am/D

Chorus   ***Repeat and fade***

Em   Bm7   Am7   Bm7 Em   Bm7   Am7/D

Get down on it,   get down on it.   Get down on it,   get down on it.

Additional Lyrics

2. I say, people, (What?)
   What you gonna do?
   You gotta get on the groove
   If you want your body to move.

Get Lucky

Words and Music by Thomas Bangalter, Guy Manuel Homem Christo,
Nile Rodgers and Pharrell Williams

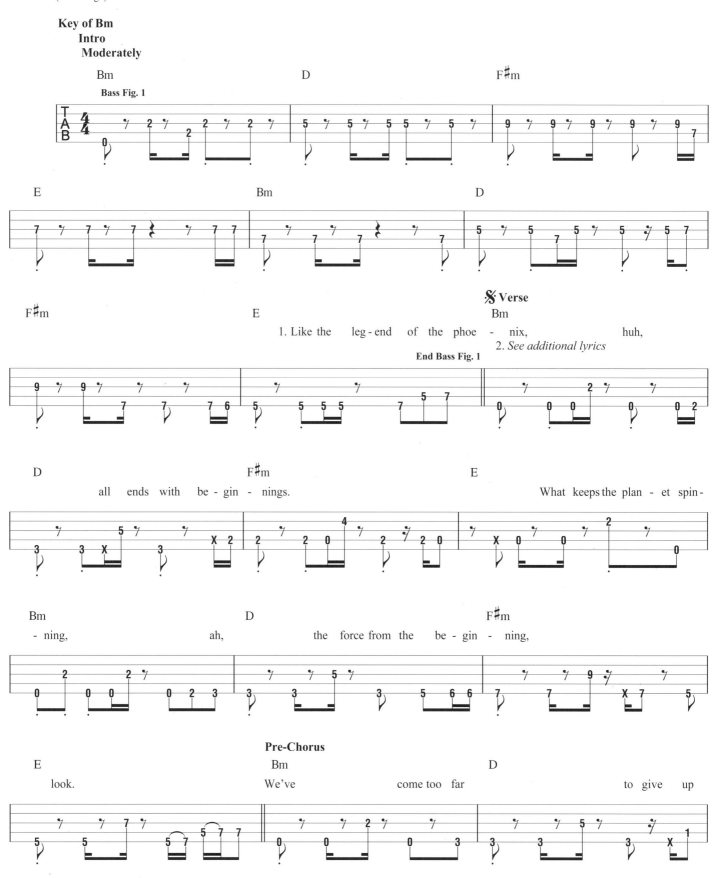

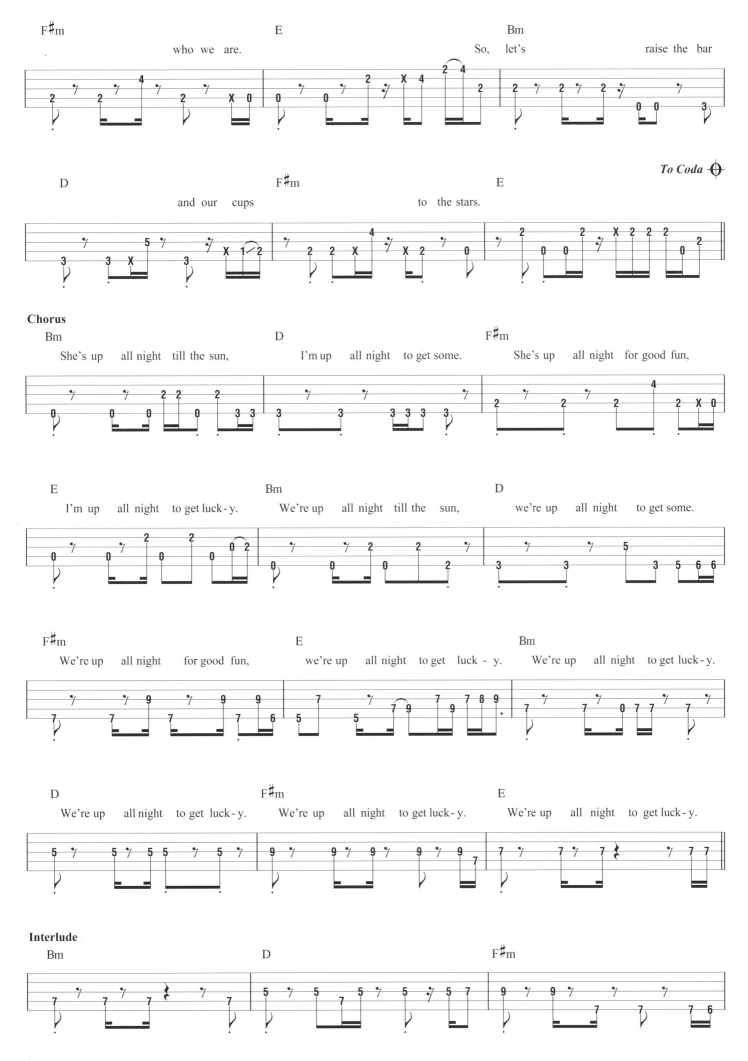

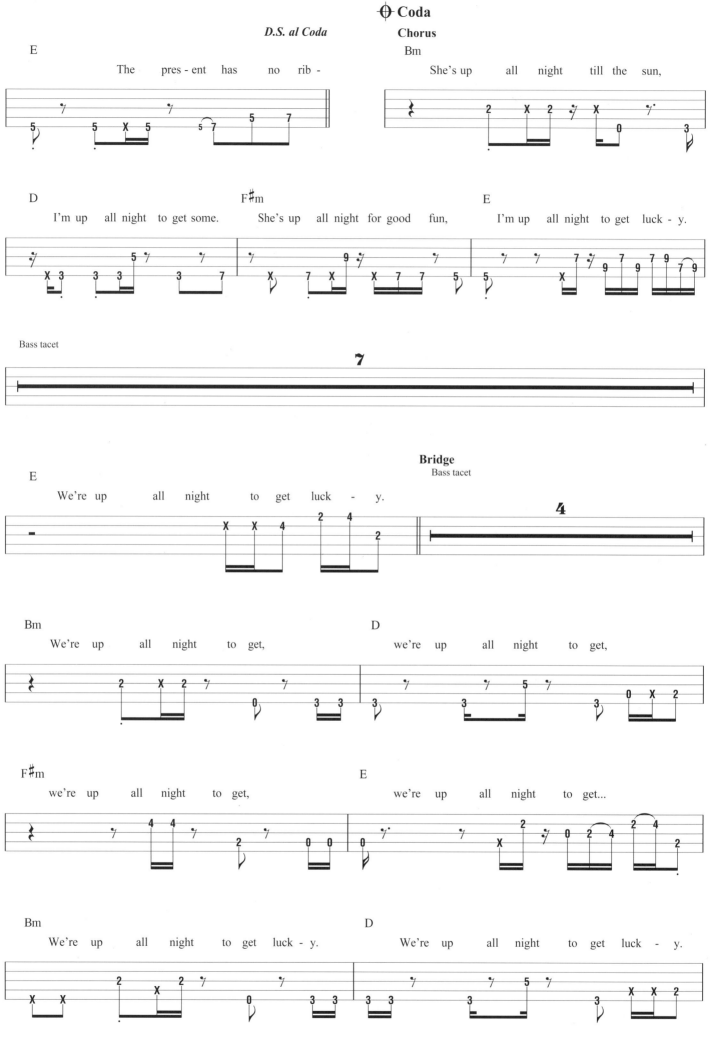

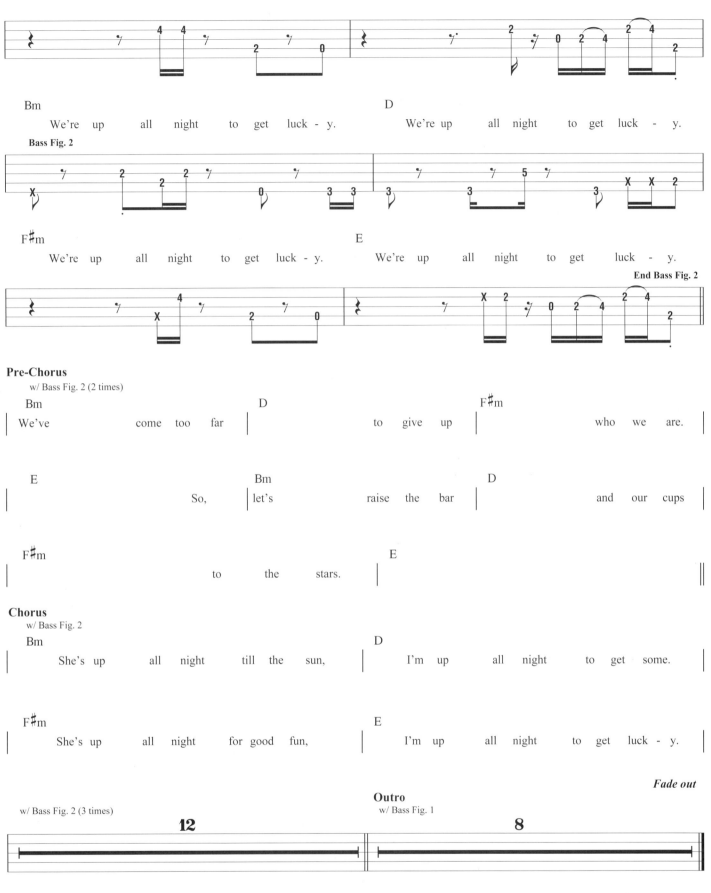

Pre-Chorus
w/ Bass Fig. 2 (2 times)

Bm | D | F#m
We've come too far | to give up | who we are.

E | Bm | D
So, let's raise the bar | and our cups

F#m | E
to the stars.

Chorus
w/ Bass Fig. 2

Bm | D
She's up all night till the sun, | I'm up all night to get some.

F#m | E
She's up all night for good fun, | I'm up all night to get luck - y.

Fade out

Outro
w/ Bass Fig. 2 (3 times)   w/ Bass Fig. 1

12   **8**

Additional Lyrics

2. The present has no ribbon.
   Your gift keeps on giving.
   What is this I'm feeling?
   If you wanna leave, I'm ready, ah.

Groove Is in the Heart

Words and Music by Kier Kirby, Dmitry Brill,
Tei Towa, Kamaal Ibn John Fareed and Herbie Hancock

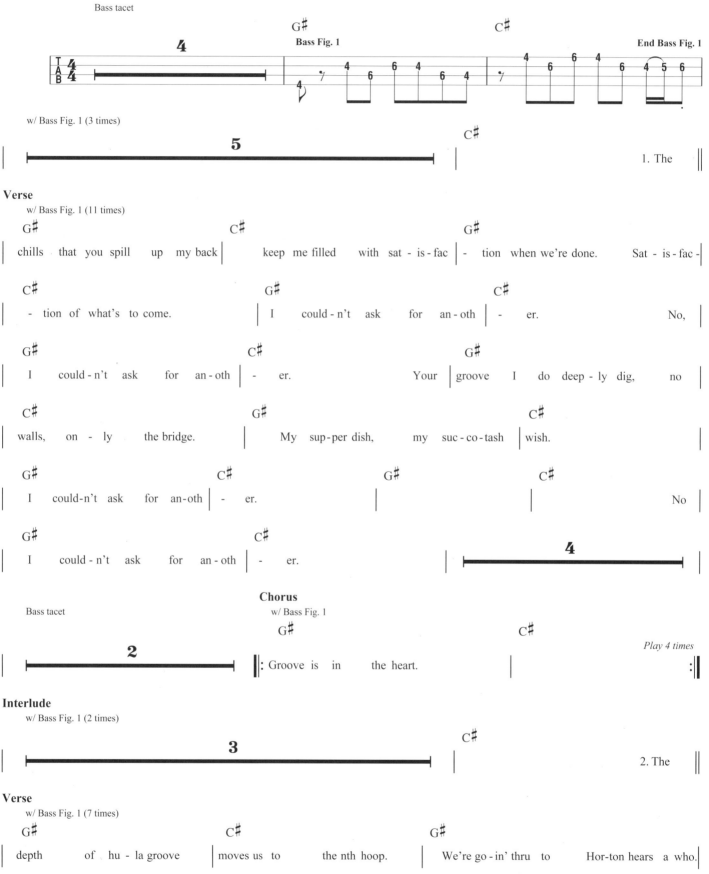

C# G# C#

I could-n't ask for an-oth | -er. No,

G# C# G#

I could-n't ask for an-oth | -er. D. J. | Soul was on a roll.

C# G# C#

I been told you can't be sold. | He's not vi-cious or ma-li-cious. | Just de-love-ly and de-li-cious.

G# C#

I could-n't ask for an-oth | -er.

Bass tacet
N.C.

2

Bridge

8

N.C.(G#)

Flow in a glow with e-lec-tric eyes. A dip to the dye, ba-by, you'll real-ize.

Bass Fig. 2

Wait 'til you see the funk-y side of me. Ba-by, you'll see that rhy-thm is a key.

Get, get with it, with it. Can't think quick-ly, quick-ly. Stomp on a stoop when I hear a funk group.

Play-in' pied pip-er. Fol-low what's true. Ba-by, just sing a-bout the groove.

End Bass Fig. 2

Chorus
w/ Bass Fig. 1 (4 times)

8

Interlude
Bass tacet

6

w/ Bass Fig. 2

8

Chorus
w/ Bass Fig. 1 (4 times)

8

Outro

G# C# G# N.C.

97

Hungry Like the Wolf

Words and Music by John Taylor, Andy Taylor, Nick Rhodes, Roger Taylor and Simon LeBon

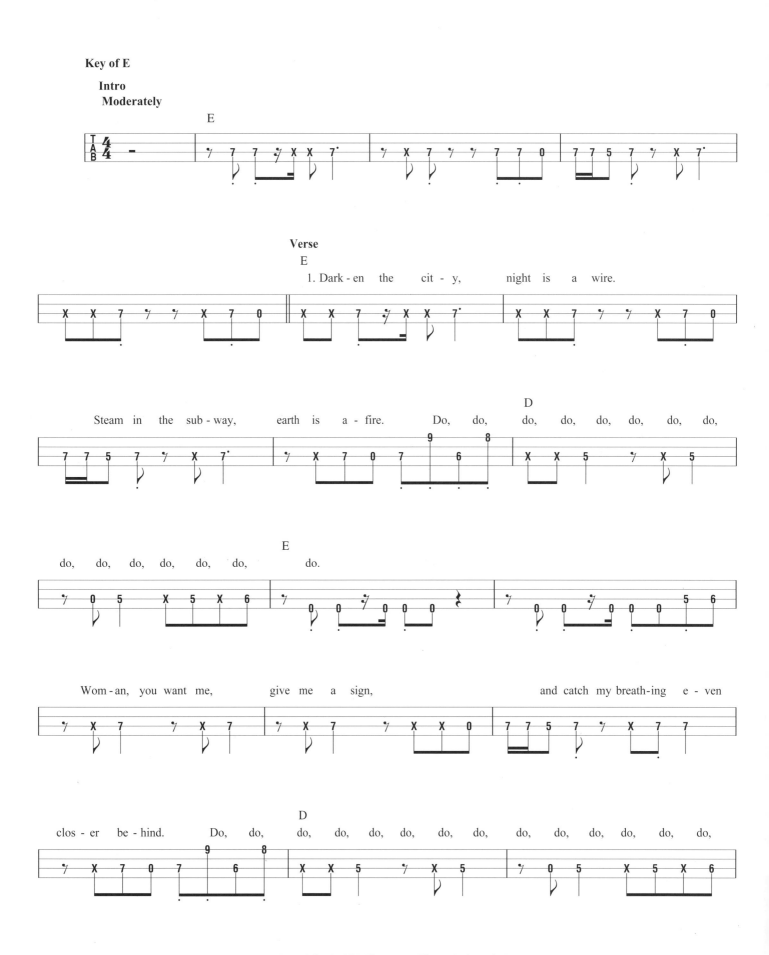

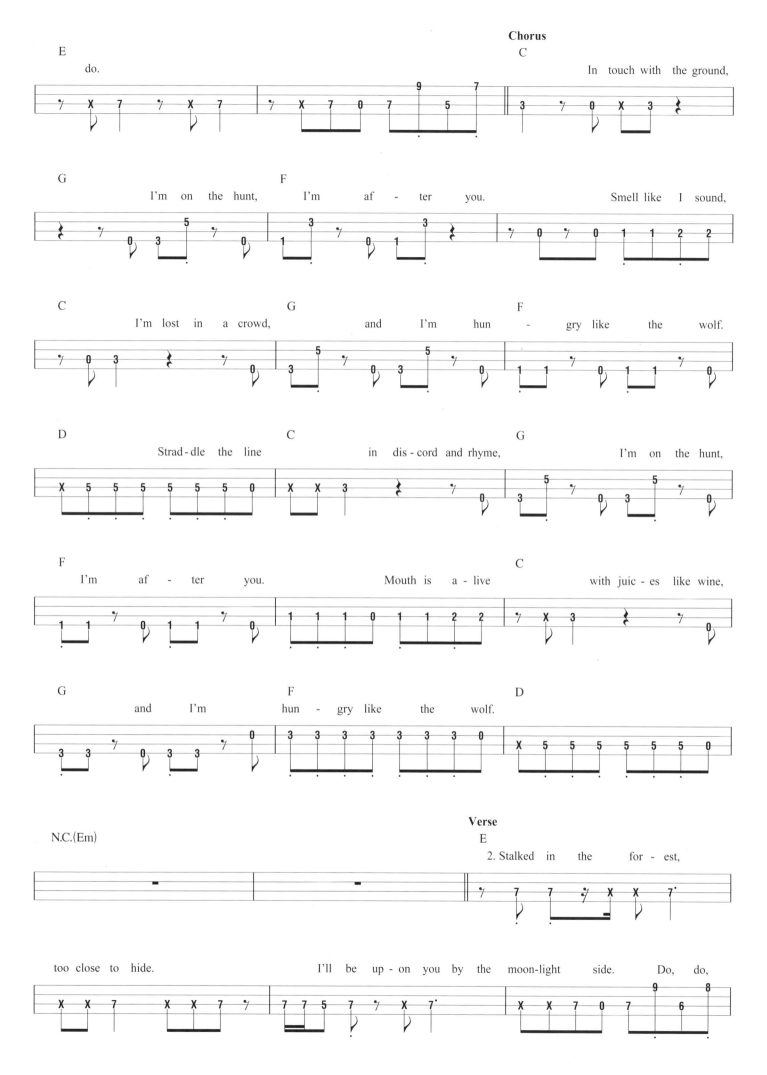

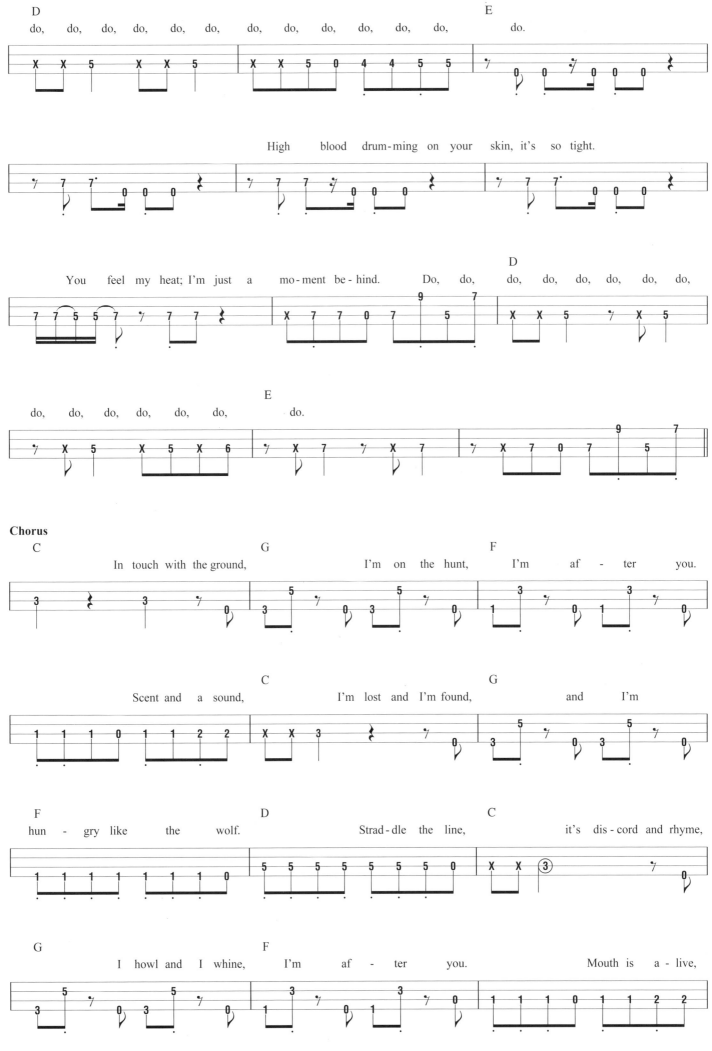

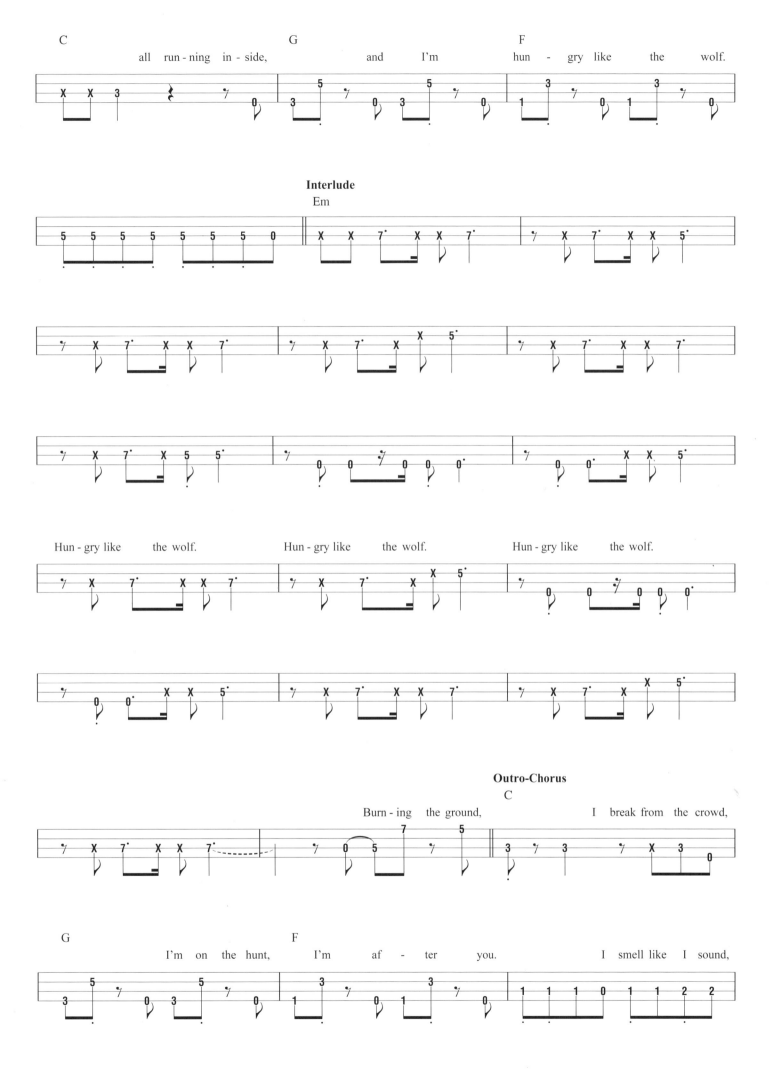

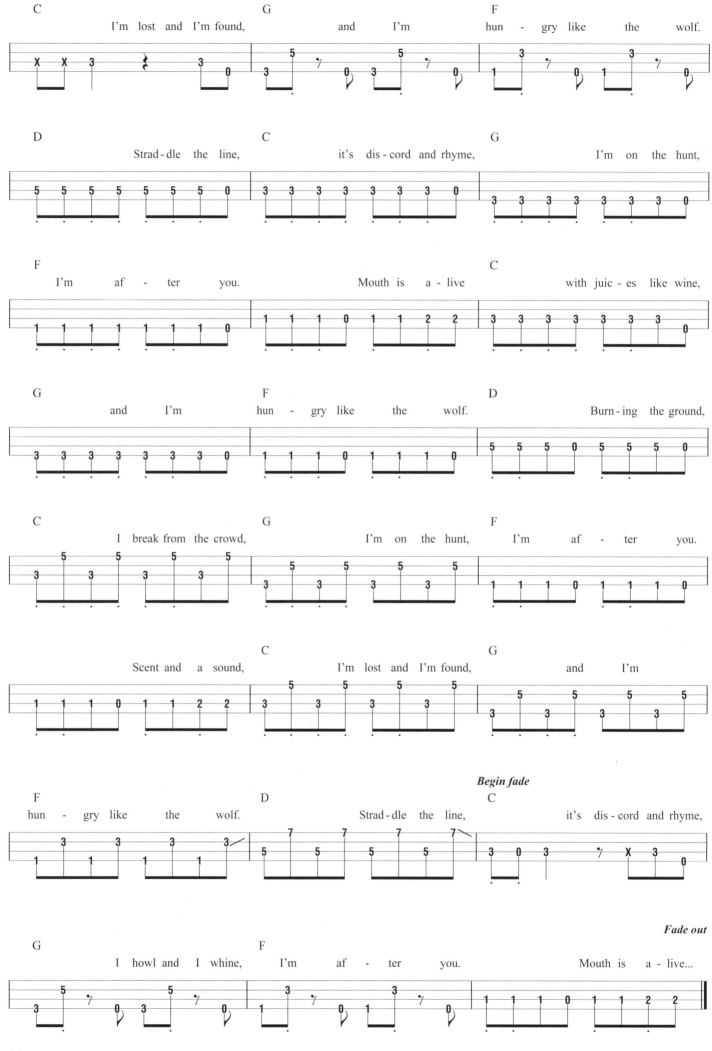

Juice

Words and Music by Lizzo, Theron Makiel Thomas, Eric Frederic, Sam Sumser and Sean Small

Key of Dm

Intro
Moderately

| 8 | | | **Verse** | 7 | |

Pre-Chorus

Dm7   F7sus4   F7

That's how I roll. If I'm shin-y, ev-'ry-bod-y gon-na shine. (Yeah, I'm

Bass Fig. 1

B♭maj7   C7   Dm7

gold.) I was born like this, don't e-ven got-ta try. (Now you know.) I'm like Char-don-nay; get

End Bass Fig. 1

F7sus4   F7   B♭maj7   C7

bet-ter o-ver time. (So you know.) Heard you say I'm not the bad-dest bitch; you lie.

𝄋 Chorus

w/ Bass Fig. 1 (3 times)

Dm7   F7sus4   F7   B♭maj7

Ain't my fault that I'm | out here get-tin' loose. Got-ta | blame it on a 'boose. Got-ta

C7   Dm7   F7sus4   F7

blame it on my juice, ba-by. Ain't my fault that I'm | out here mak-in' news. I'm the

B♭maj7   C7   Dm7

pud-din' in the proof. Got-ta | blame it on my juice. Ya, ya, | ee, ya, yi,

To Coda ⊕

F7sus4   F7   B♭maj7   C7

ya, yi, ya, ya... | Blame it on my juice. Blame it, | blame it on my juice. Ya, ya,

Bridge

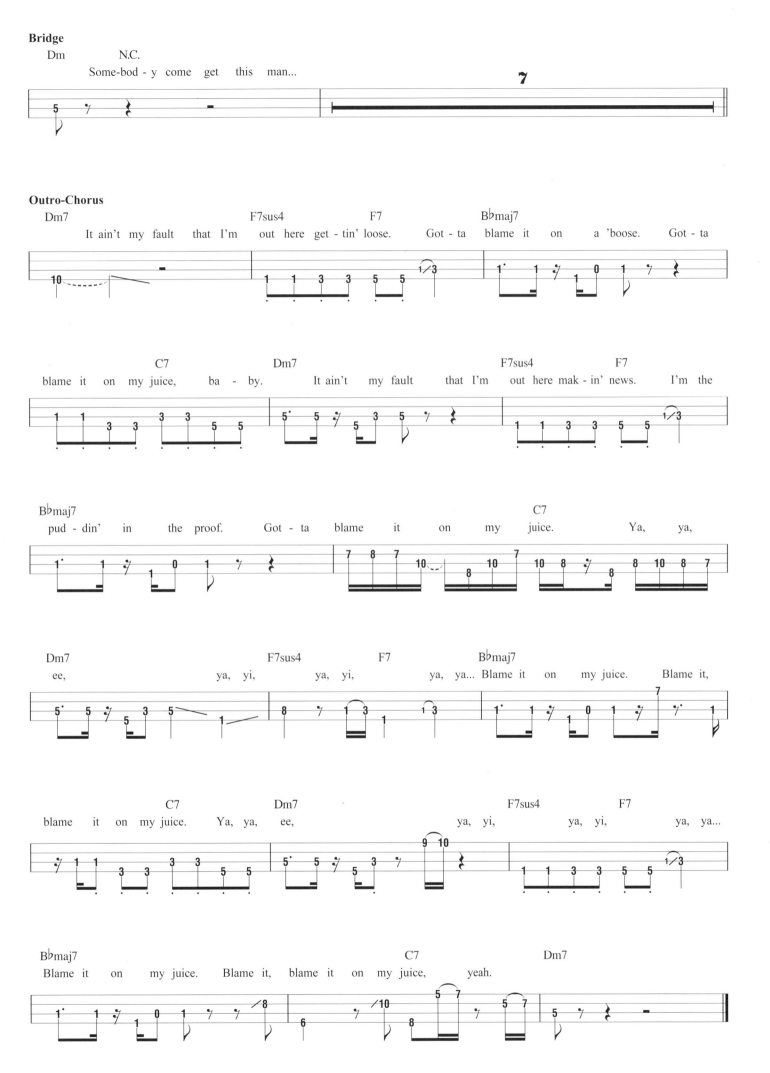

Outro-Chorus

I Melt With You

Words and Music by Richard Ian Brown, Michael Francis Conroy,
Robert James Grey, Gary Frances McDowell and Stephen James Walker

Key of C

Intro
Moderately

Bass Fig. 1

End Bass Fig. 1

w/ pick

Verse

1. Mov-ing for - wards, us-ing all my breath.
2. *See additional lyrics*

Mak-ing love to you was nev-er sec - ond best.

I saw the world crash-ing all a - round your face,

nev-er real-ly know - ing it was al - ways mesh and lace.

Chorus

w/ Bass Fig. 1 (4 times)

I'll stop the world and melt with you.

1., 2. You've seen the dif - f'rence and it's } get - ting bet - ter all the time.
3. I've seen some chang - es but it's }

There's noth-ing you and I won't do.

I'll stop the world and melt with you.

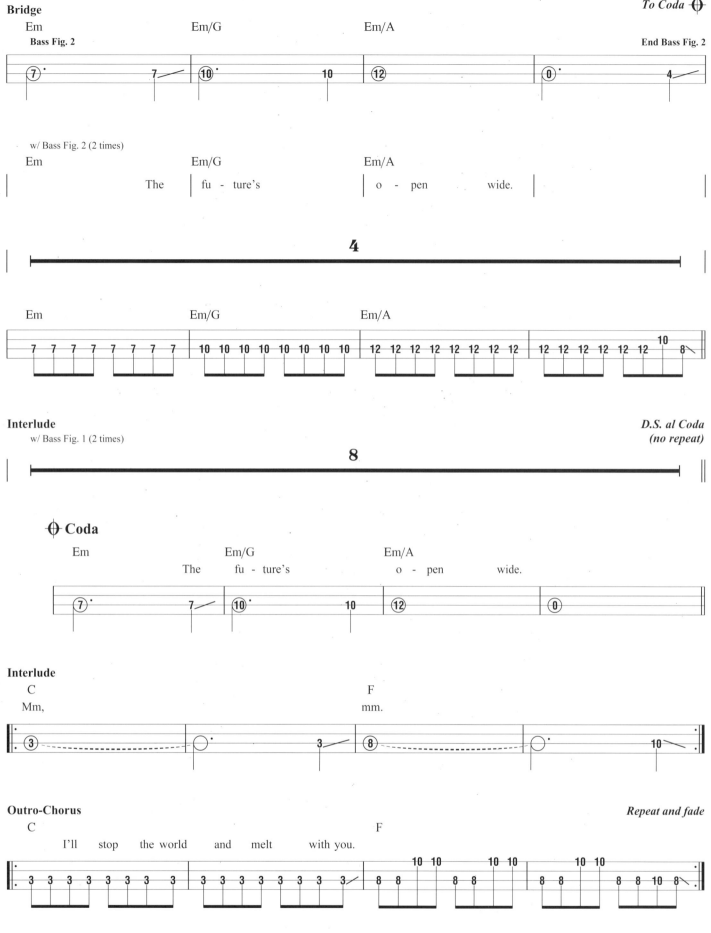

Additional Lyrics

2. Dream of better lives, the kind which never hate.
Trapped in a state of imaginary grace.
I made a pilgrimage to save this human's race.
Never comprehending the race had long gone by.

I Wanna Dance With Somebody

Words and Music by George Merrill and Shannon Rubicam

5-string bass:
(low to high) B-E-A-D-G

Key of F♯

Intro
Moderately

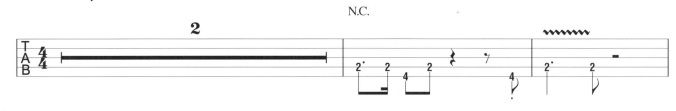

F♯

D♯m7

Bmaj7   G♯m7 A♯m7 B6 C♯11   F♯

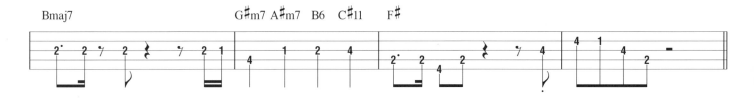

𝄉 Verse

C♯   D♯m

1. The clock strikes up - on the hour and the sun be - gins to fade.
2. *See additional lyrics*

C♯

There's still e - nough time to fig - ure out how to

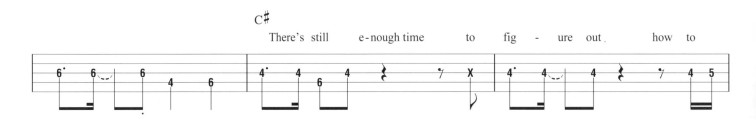

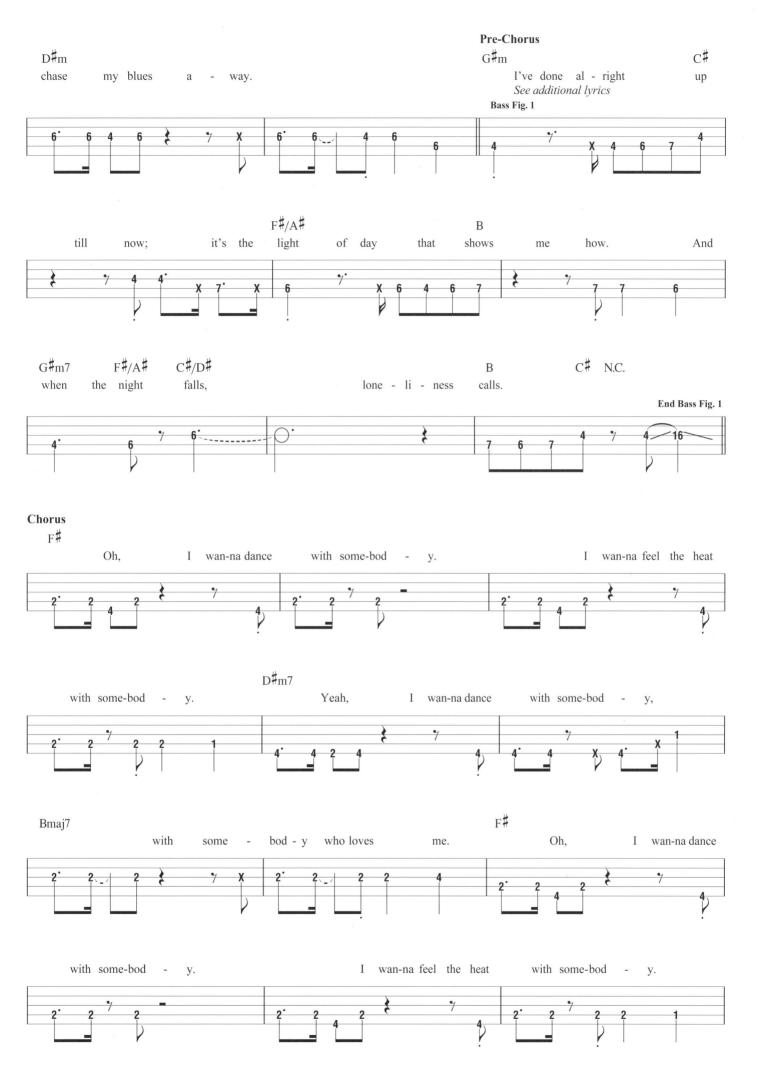

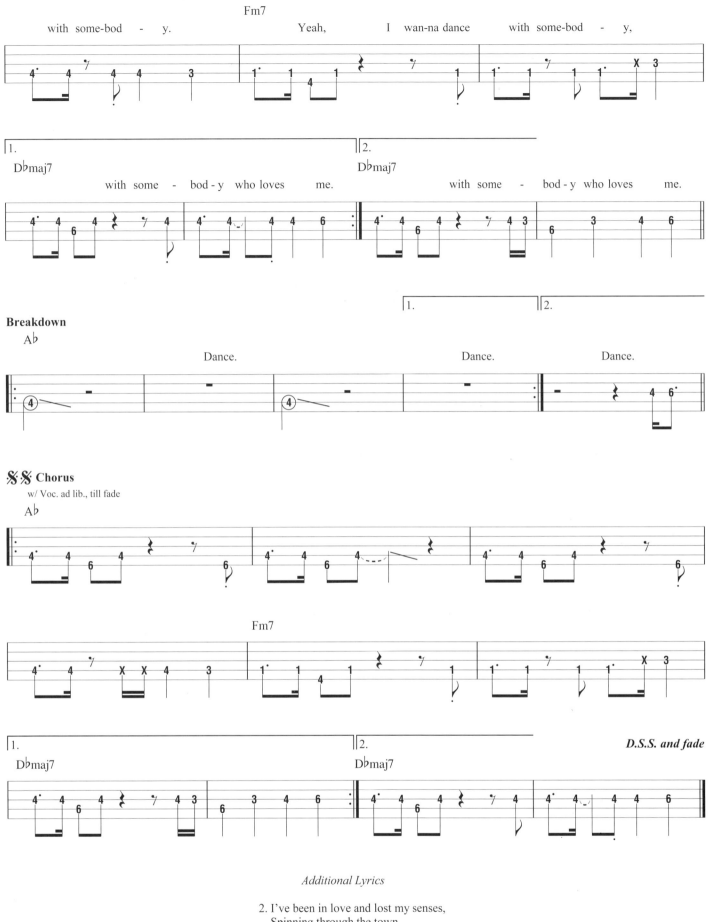

Additional Lyrics

2. I've been in love and lost my senses,
   Spinning through the town.
   Sooner or later the fever ends,
   And I wind up feeling down.

Pre-Chorus I need a man who'll take a chance
   On a love that burns hot enough to last.
   So when the night falls, my lonely heart calls.

Let's Get It Started

Words and Music by Will Adams, Allan Pineda, Jaime Gomez,
Michael Fratantuno, George Pajon Jr. and Terence Yoshiaki Graves

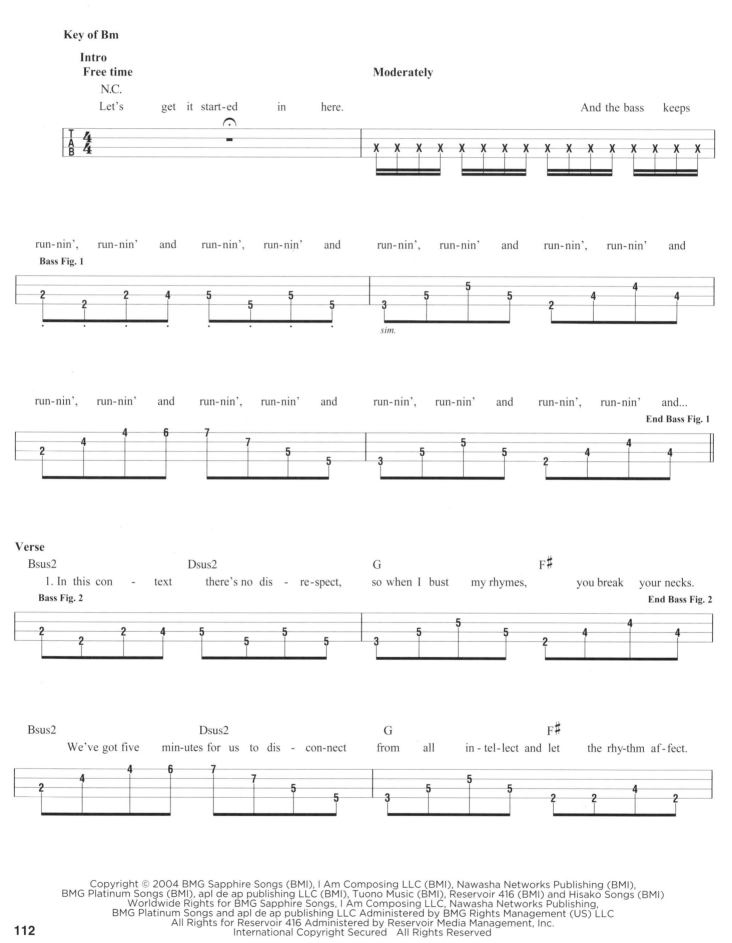

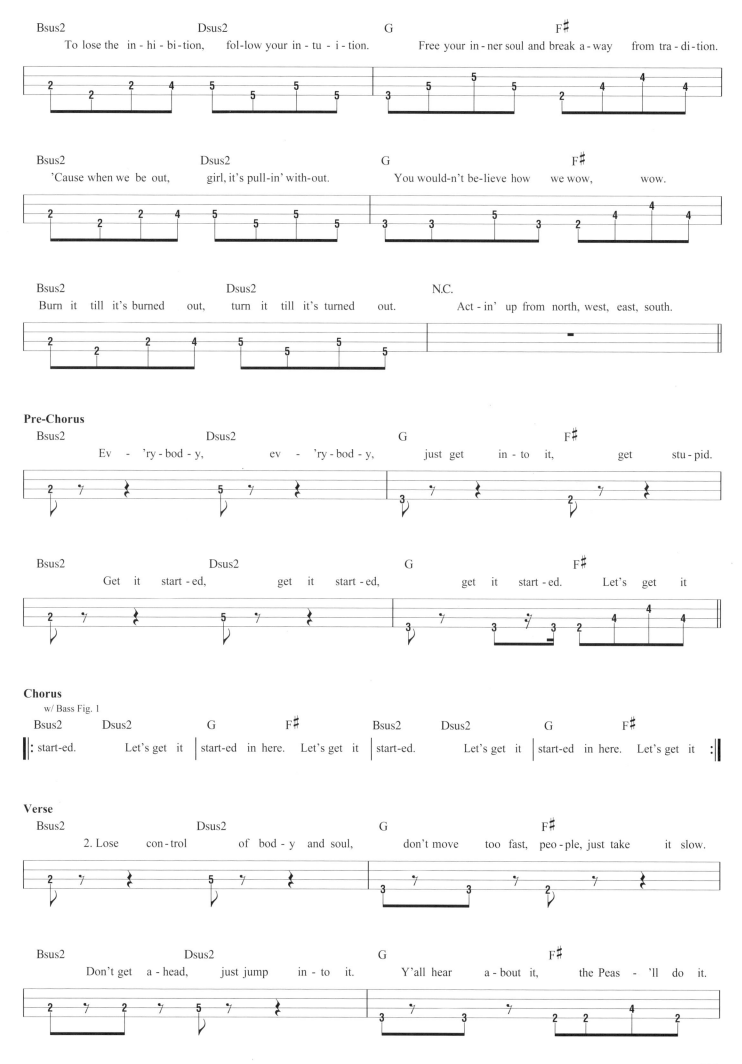

w/ Bass Fig. 2 (3 times)

Bsus2   Dsus2   G   F#

Get start-ed, get stu-pid, | don't wor - ry 'bout it, peo-ple, we'll walk you through it. |

Bsus2   Dsus2   G   F#

Step by step, like a in-fant, new kid. | Inch by inch, with the new so-lu - tion. |

Bsus2   Dsus2   G   F#

Trans - mit hits with no de-lu - sion, the | feel-ing's ir - re-sist - i - ble and that's how we move it. ‖

Pre-Chorus

Bsus2   Dsus2   G   F#

Ev - 'ry-bod - y, ev - 'ry-bod - y, just get in-to it and get stu -

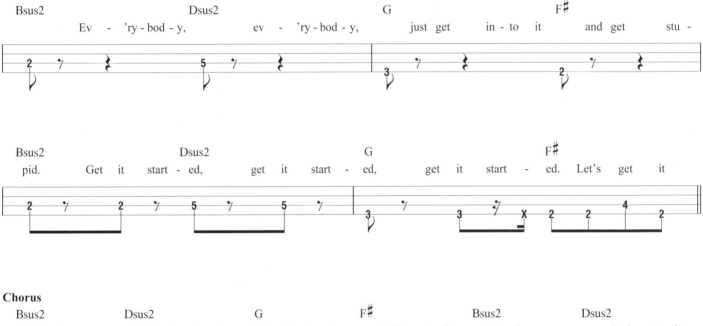

Bsus2   Dsus2   G   F#

pid. Get it start - ed, get it start - ed, get it start - ed. Let's get it

Chorus

Bsus2   Dsus2   G   F#   Bsus2   Dsus2

start - ed. Let's get it start - ed in here. Let's get it start - ed. Let's get it

Bass Fig. 3

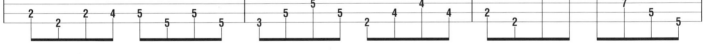

G   F#   Bsus2   Dsus2   G   F#

start - ed in here. Let's get it start - ed. Let's get it start - ed in here. Let's get it

End Bass Fig. 3

Bsus2   Dsus2   G   F#

start - ed. Let's get it start - ed in here. And the bass keeps

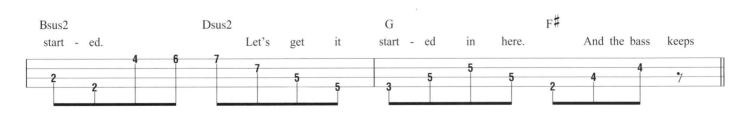

Interlude

N.C.

run-nin', run-nin' and run-nin', run-nin' and   run-nin', run-nin' and run-nin', run-nin' and,

```
|x x x x x x x x x x x x|x x x x x x x x x x x x|
```

Bsus2   G   Dsus2   F♯   Bsus2   G   Dsus2   F♯

oo. (Uh-huh.) We cuck - oo, (in here.) We cuck - oo. (Uh-huh.) We cuck - oo, (in here.) We cuck -

```
|2   2   2  5  5 5|  5 5 5  4  4 4|2   2   2  5  5 5|  5  5 5⁵7  4  4 4|
|  2   2   2      |  5 5 5         |  2   2   2      |     5         4  |
```

Bsus2   G   Dsus2   F♯   G   A   F♯5

oo. (Uh-huh.) We cuck - oo, (in here.)   Ya, ya, ya, ya, ya, ya, ya,   ya, ya, ya, ya, ya, ya, ya, ya,

```
|2   2   2  5  5 5|  5 5 5  4  4 4|3 3 3 3 3 3 3 3|5 5 5 5⟍2 2 2 2|
|  2   2   2      |  5 5 5         |               |              |
```

Bridge

Bsus2

ya. Let's get ill, that's the deal.   At the gate, we'll bring the bud, top drill. (Just)

Bass Fig. 4   End Bass Fig. 4

```
|2  ᶎ  ᶎ  2  2  ᶎ  𝄽|2  ᶎ  ᶎ  2  2  ᶎ  𝄽|
```

w/ Bass Fig. 4 (2 times)

lose your mind, this is the time, y'all | guessed this ill just to bang your spine. (Just)

bob your head like me, Ap - ple Dee, | up in - side your club or in your Bent - ley.

Dsus2   G   F♯

Get mess-y, loud and sick, your mind past nor - mal on an - oth - er head trip. So,

```
|2  ᶎ  ᶎ  2  5  ᶎ  ᶎ  5|3  ᶎ  ᶎ    3  2  ᶎ  ᶎ    2|
```

Bsus2   Dsus2   G   F♯

come then now, do not cor - rect it,   let's get ig - 'nant, let's get hec - tic.

```
|2  ᶎ  ᶎ  2  5  ᶎ  ᶎ  5|3  ᶎ    3  2  ᶎ  2  ᶎ|
```

Pre-Chorus

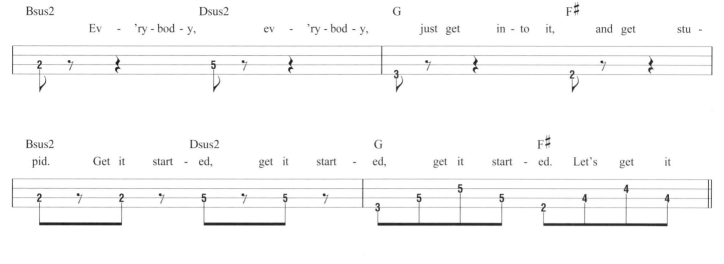

Bsus2   Dsus2   G   F#

Ev - 'ry-bod - y,   ev - 'ry-bod - y,   just get in - to it,   and get stu -

Bsus2   Dsus2   G   F#

pid.   Get it start - ed,   get it start - ed,   get it start - ed. Let's get it

Chorus

w/ Bass Fig. 1

Bsus2   Dsus2   G   F#   Bsus2   Dsus2   G   F#

start-ed.   Let's get it | start-ed in here. Let's get it | start-ed.   Let's get it | start-ed in here. Let's get it |

w/ Bass Fig. 3

Bsus2   Dsus2   G   F#   Bsus2   Dsus2   G   F#

start-ed.   Let's get it | start-ed in here. Let's get it | start-ed.   Let's get it | start-ed in here. We cuck - ||

Outro

Bsus2   G   Dsus2   F#   Bsus2   G   Dsus2   F#

oo. (Uh-huh.) We cuck - oo, (in here.) We cuck - oo. (Uh-huh.) We cuck - oo, (in here.)

Bass tacet

N.C.

Run-nin',   run-nin' and   run-nin', run-nin' and | run-nin', run-nin' and   run-nin', run-nin' and |

G5   A5   F#5

run-nin',   run-nin' and   run-nin', run-nin' and   run-nin', run-nin' and   run-nin', run-nin' and

Repeat and fade

B5   N.C.

run-nin',   run-nin' and   run-nin', run-nin' and   run-nin', run-nin' and   run-nin', run-nin' and

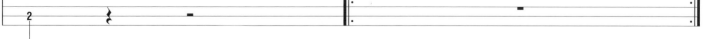

Love Shack

Words and Music by Catherine E. Pierson, Frederick W. Schneider,
Keith J. Strickland and Cynthia L. Wilson

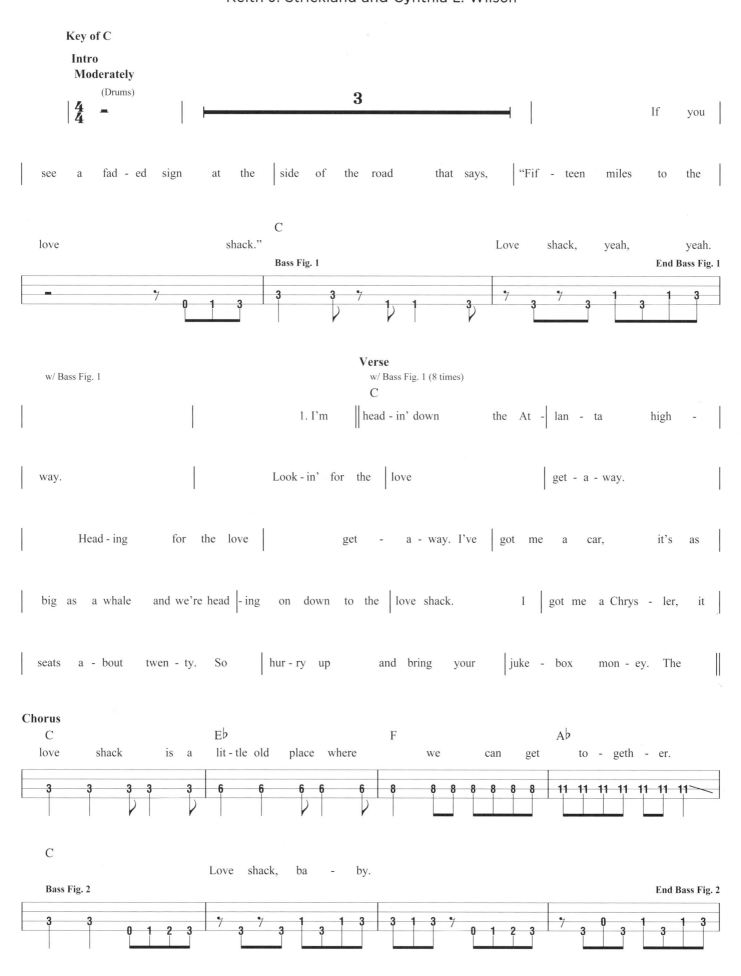

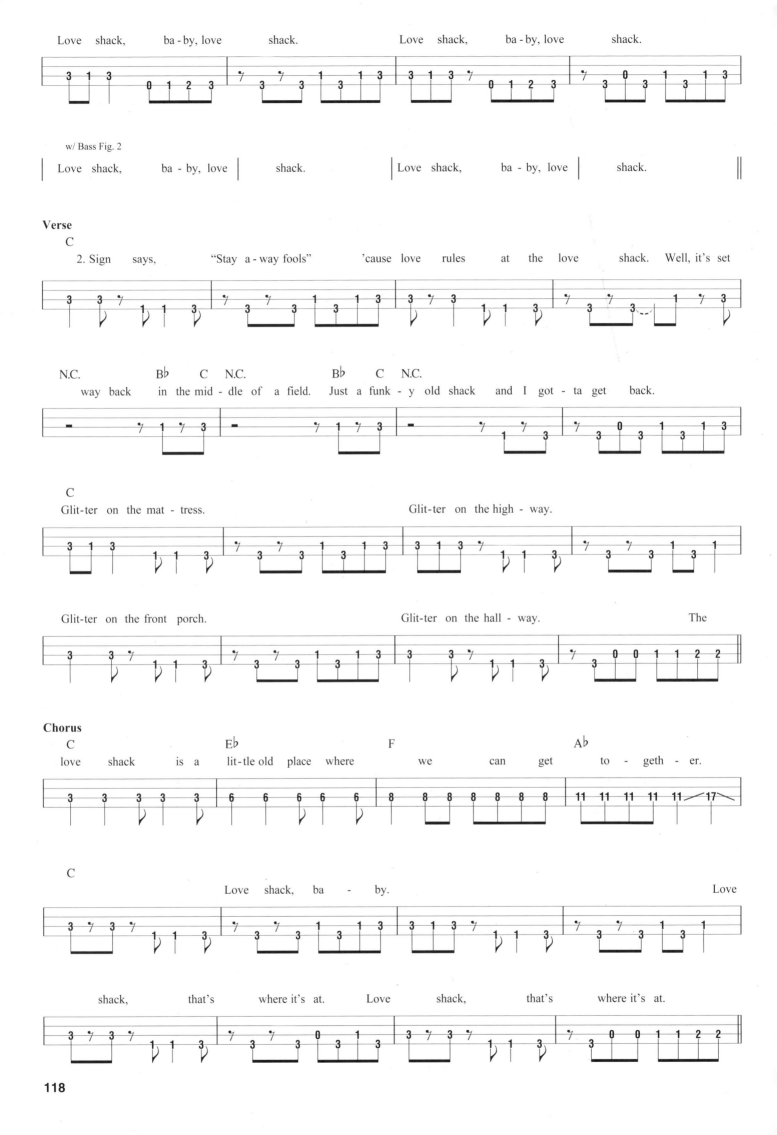

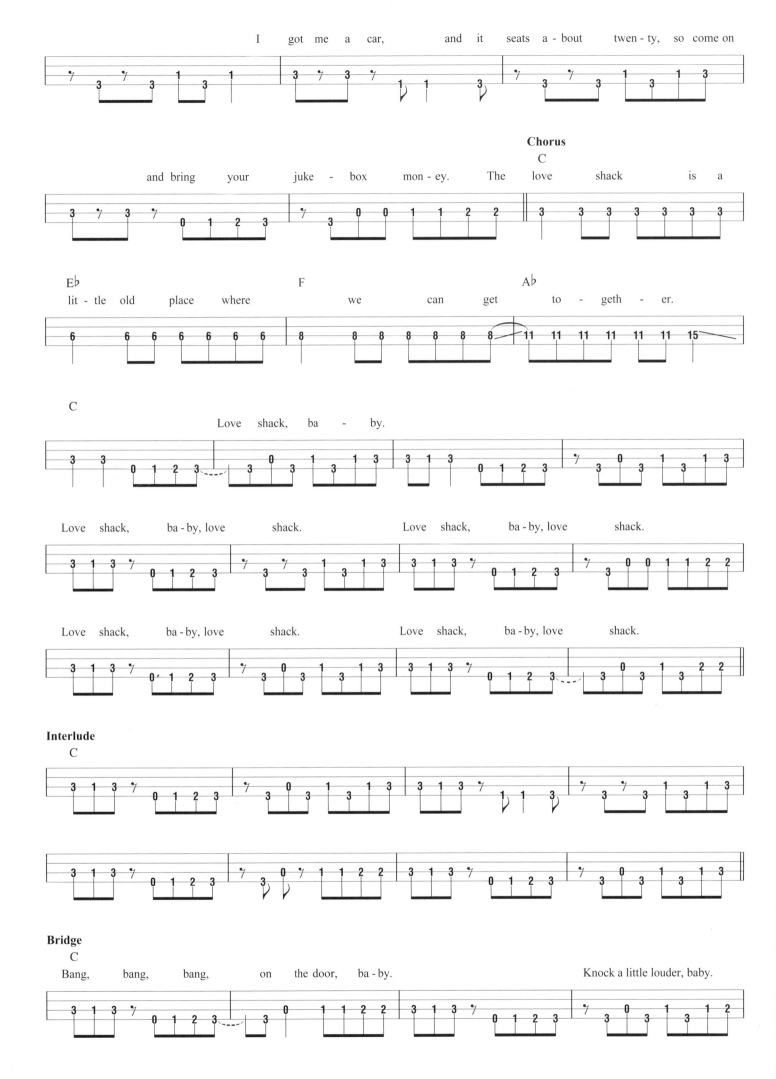

Chorus

Interlude

Bridge

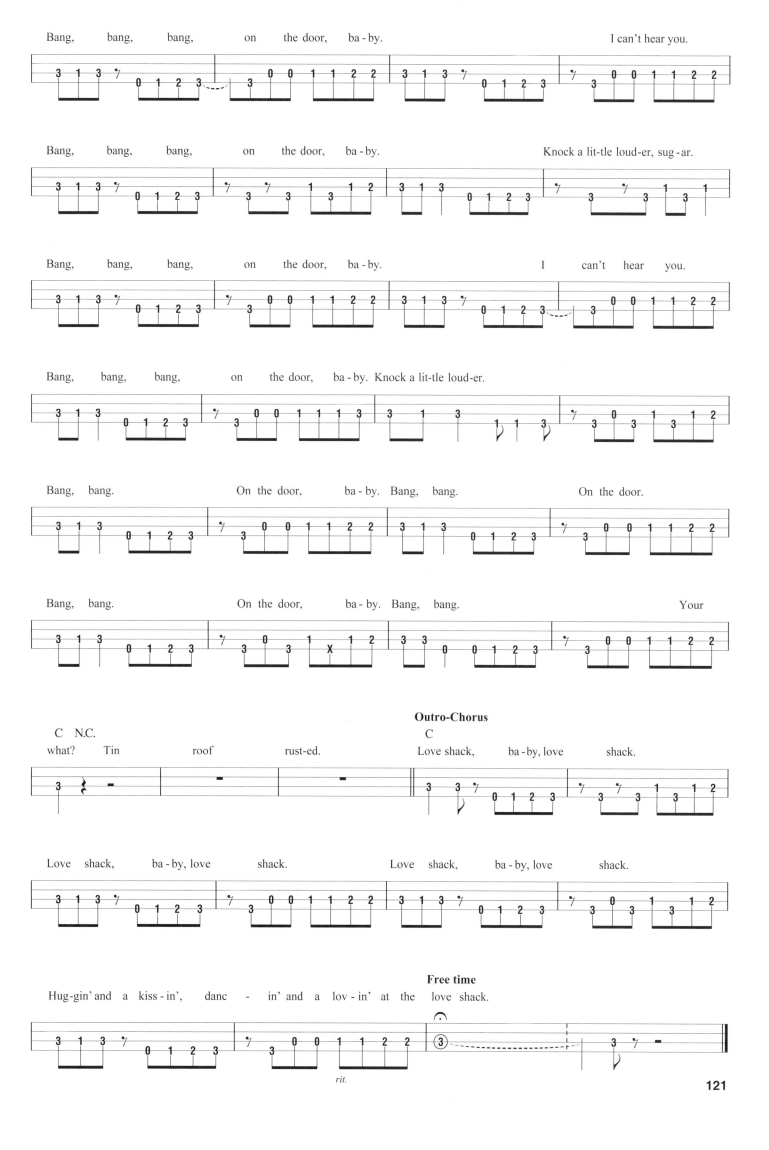

Mr. Brightside

Words and Music by Brandon Flowers, Dave Keuning, Mark Stoermer and Ronnie Vannucci

Tune down 1/2 step:
(low to high) Eb-Ab-Db-Gb

Key of D

Intro
Moderately fast

(Guitar)

Verse
Bass tacet

D / D/C#
1. Com - in' out - ta my cage and I've been do - in' just

Gmaj7
fine. Got - ta, got - ta be down be - cause I want it all.

D / D/C# / Gmaj7
It start - ed out with a kiss. How did it end up like this? It was on - ly a kiss,

D / D/C#
it was on - ly a kiss. Now I'm fall - ing a - sleep, and she's call - ing a cab

Bass Fig. 1

Gmaj7 / D
while he's hav - in' a smoke and she's tak - in' a drag. Now they're go - ing to bed

D/C# / G
and my stom - ach is sick. And it's all in my head, but she's touch - ing his

End Bass Fig. 1

% Pre-Chorus

Bm7 / Bm7/A
chest. Now he takes off her dress. Now let me

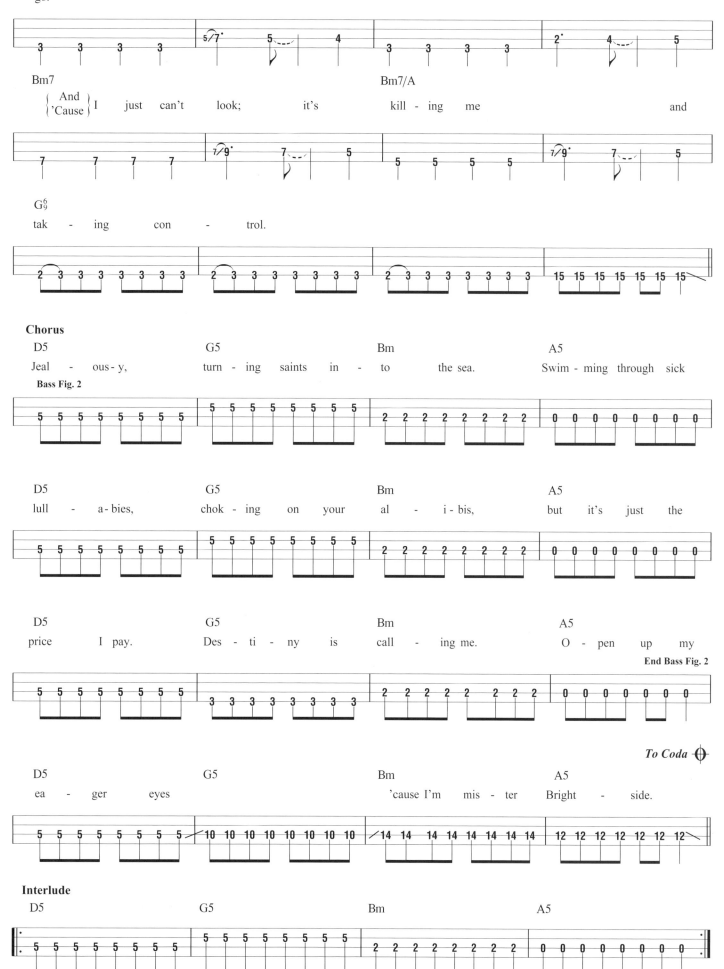

Verse

w/ Bass Fig. 1 (1st 4 meas.)

D   D/C#
　　2. I'm com - in' out - ta my cage　　　and I've been do - in' just

Gmaj7
　　fine. Got - ta, got - ta be down　　　be - cause I want it all.

D   D/C#
　　It start - ed out with a　　　kiss. How did it end up like

Gmaj7
　　this? (It was on - ly a kiss.)　　　It was on - ly a kiss.

w/ Bass Fig. 1

D   D/C#
　　Now I'm fall - ing a - sleep,　　　and she's call - ing a cab

Gmaj7
　　while he's hav - ing a smoke　　　and she's tak - ing a drag.

D   D/C#
　　Now they're go - ing to bed　　　and my stom - ach is sick.

D.S. al Coda

Gmaj7
　　And it's all in my head,　　　but she's touch - ing his

Coda

Interlude

D   G5   Bm   A   D   G5

Bm   A

Outro

w/ Bass Fig. 2

D5   G5   Bm   A5   *Play 3 times*
: nev - er.   I :

D5   G5   Bm   A5
nev - er.

124

Rude

Words and Music by Nasri Atweh, Mark Pellizzer, Alex Tanas, Ben Spivak and Adam Messinger

Key of D♭

Verse

Slow

1. Sat - ur - day morn - ing, jumped out of bed and put on my best suit.

Got in my car and raced like a jet all the way to you.

Knocked on your door with heart in my hand to ask you a ques - tion,

'cause I know that you're an old fash - ioned man, yeah.

Pre-Chorus

Can I have your daugh-ter for the rest of my life? Say yes, say yes, 'cause I need to know. You say I'll

nev - er get your bless-ing 'til the day I die. "Tough luck, my friend, but the an - swer is no." / 'cause the an - swer's still no."

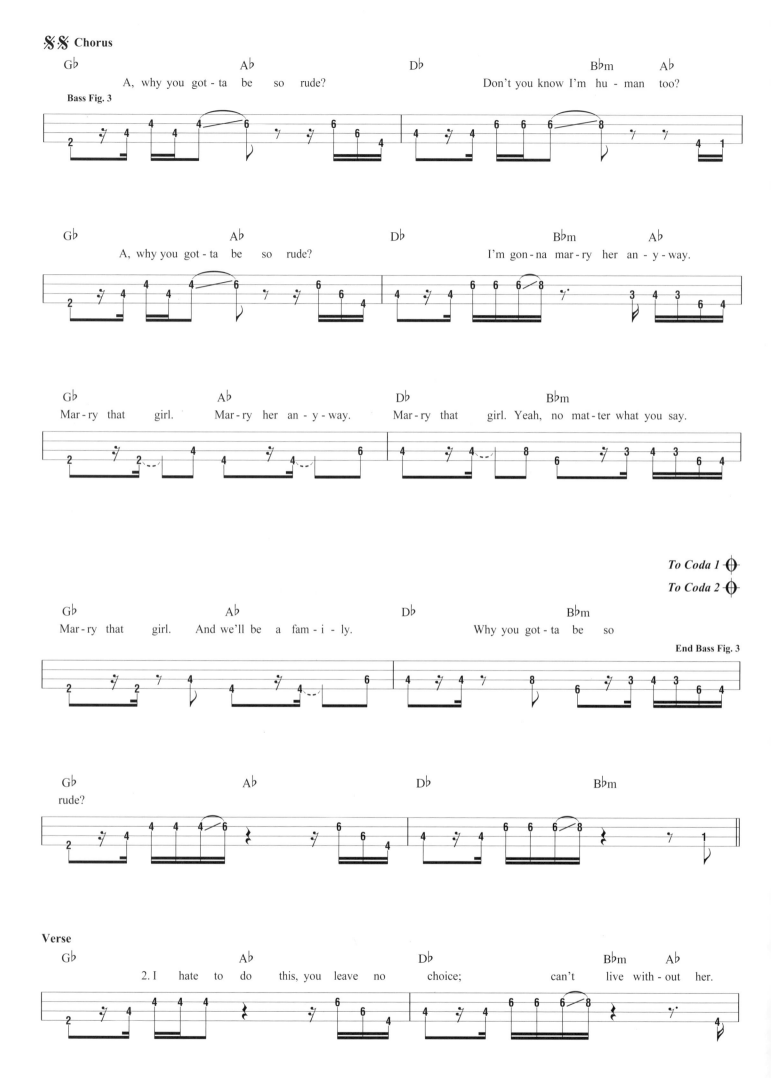

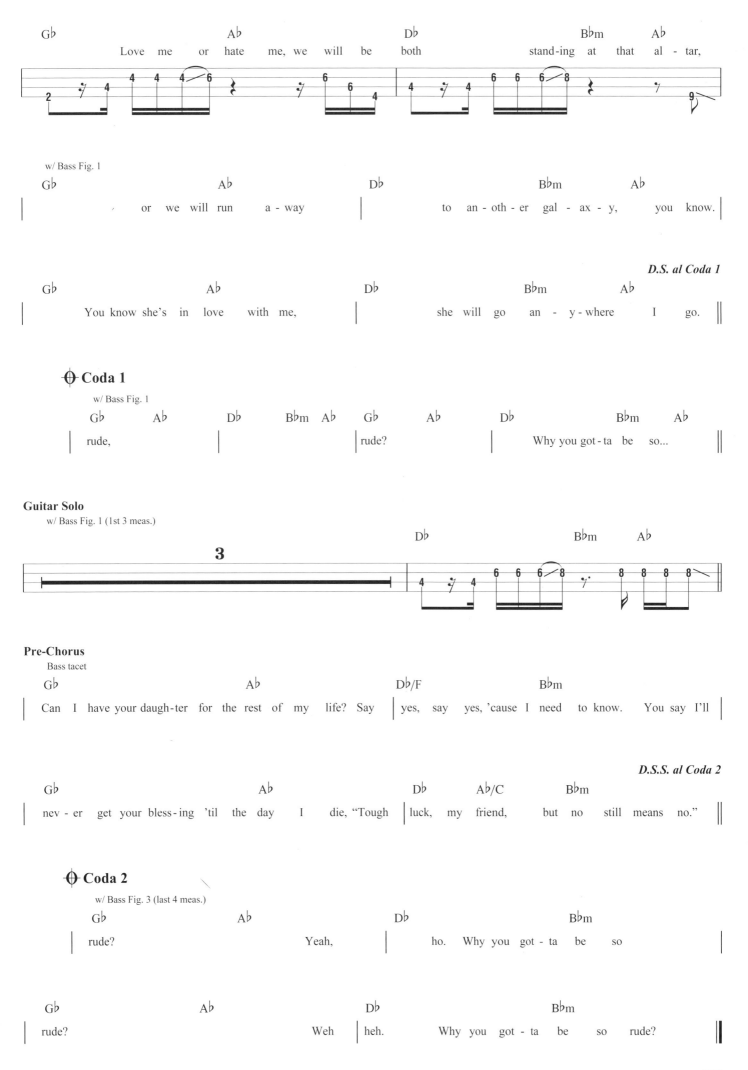

My Sharona

Words and Music by Doug Fieger and Berton Averre

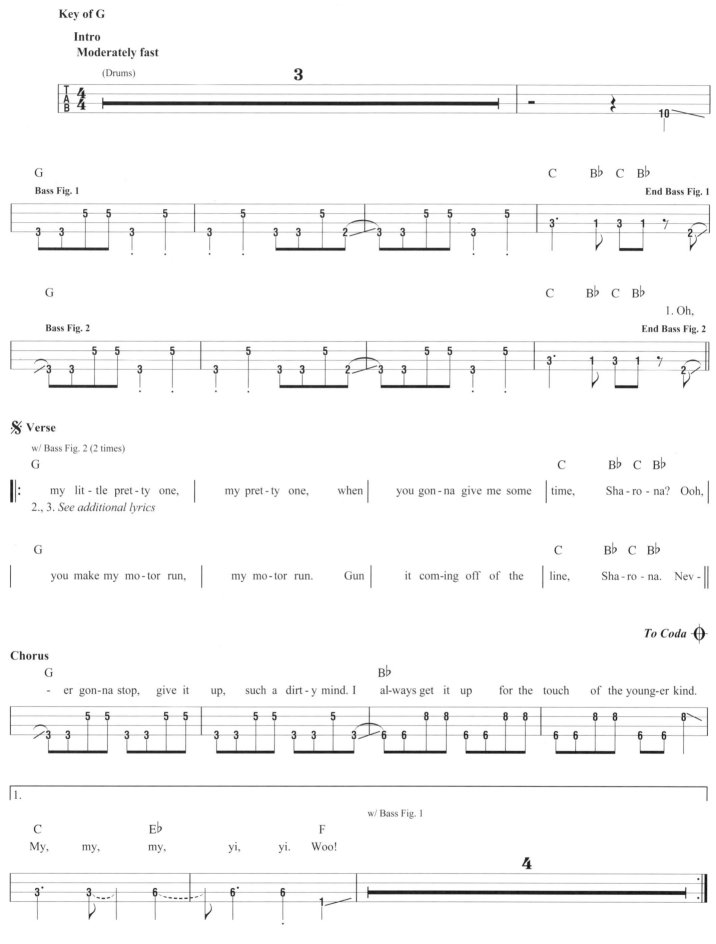

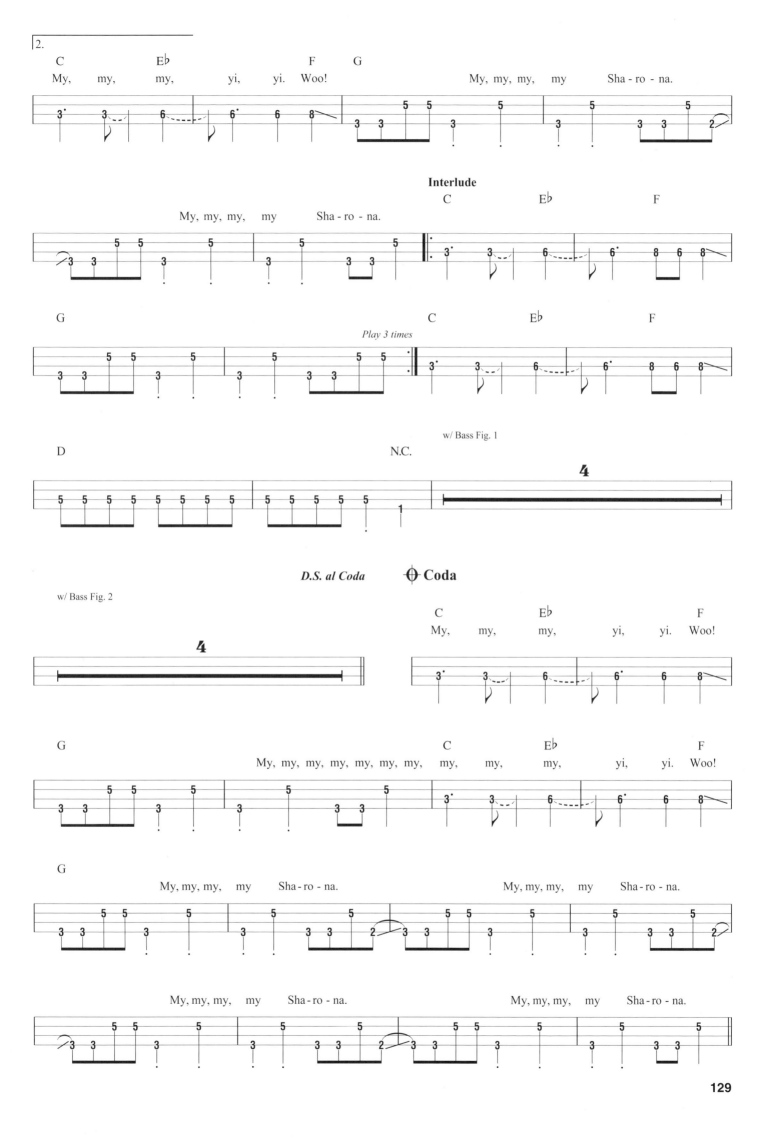

Interlude

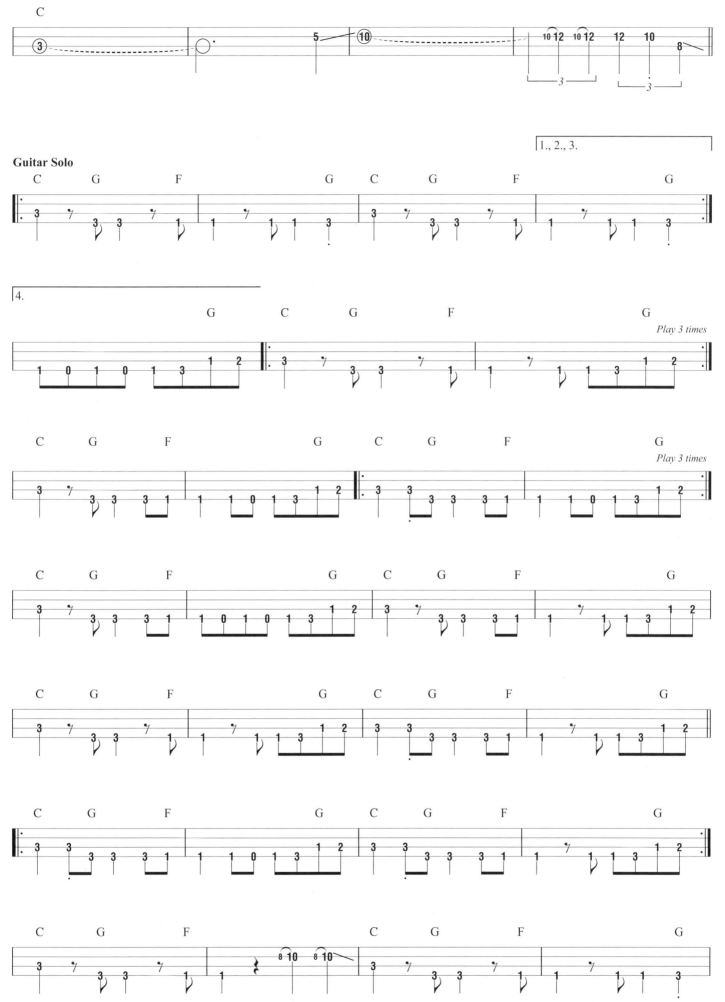

Guitar Solo

130

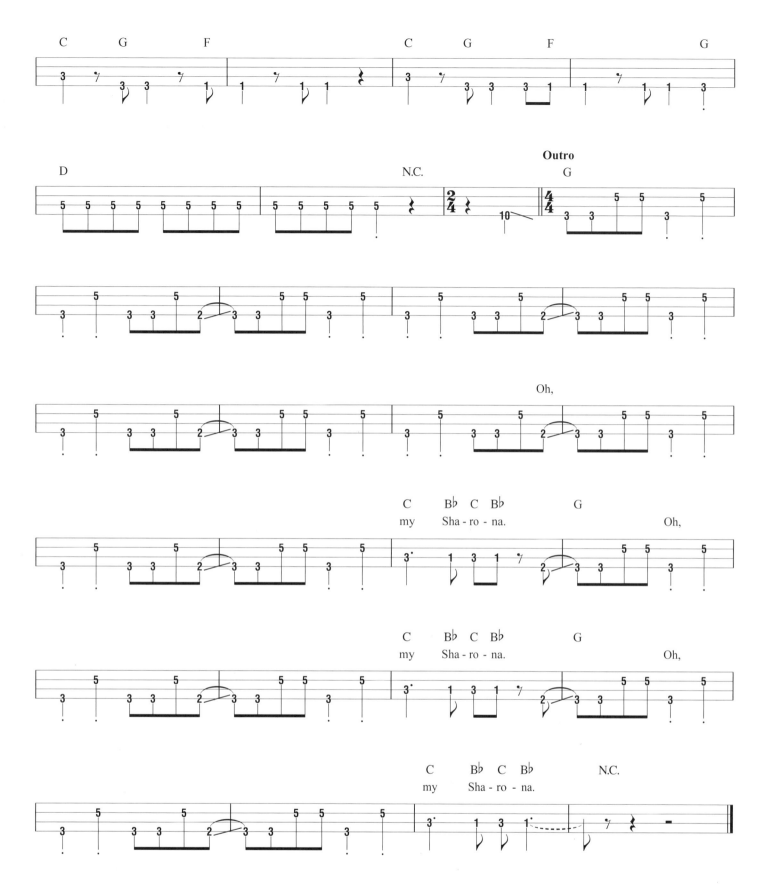

Additional Lyrics

2. Come a little closer, huh, uh, will ya, huh?
   Close enough to look in my eyes, Sharona.
   Keeping it a mystery, it gets to me.
   Running down the length of my thigh, Sharona.

3. When you gonna give to me, g-give to me,
   Is it just a matter of time, Sharona?
   Is it d-d-destiny, d-destiny,
   Or is it just a game in my mind, Sharona?

Orphans

Words and Music by Guy Berryman, Jon Buckland, Will Champion, Chris Martin and Moses Martin

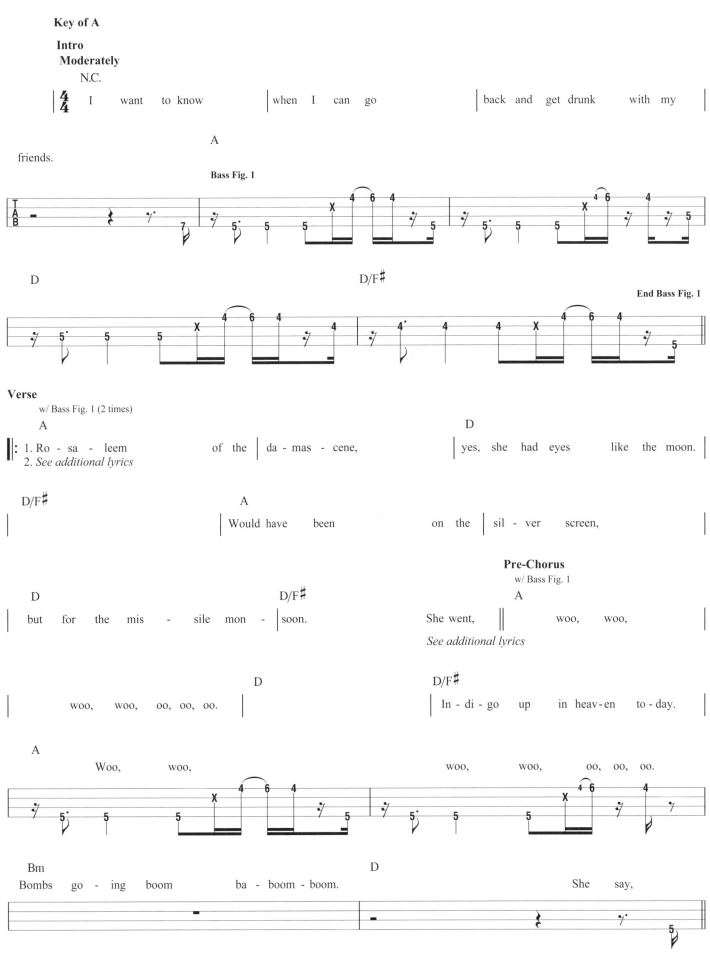

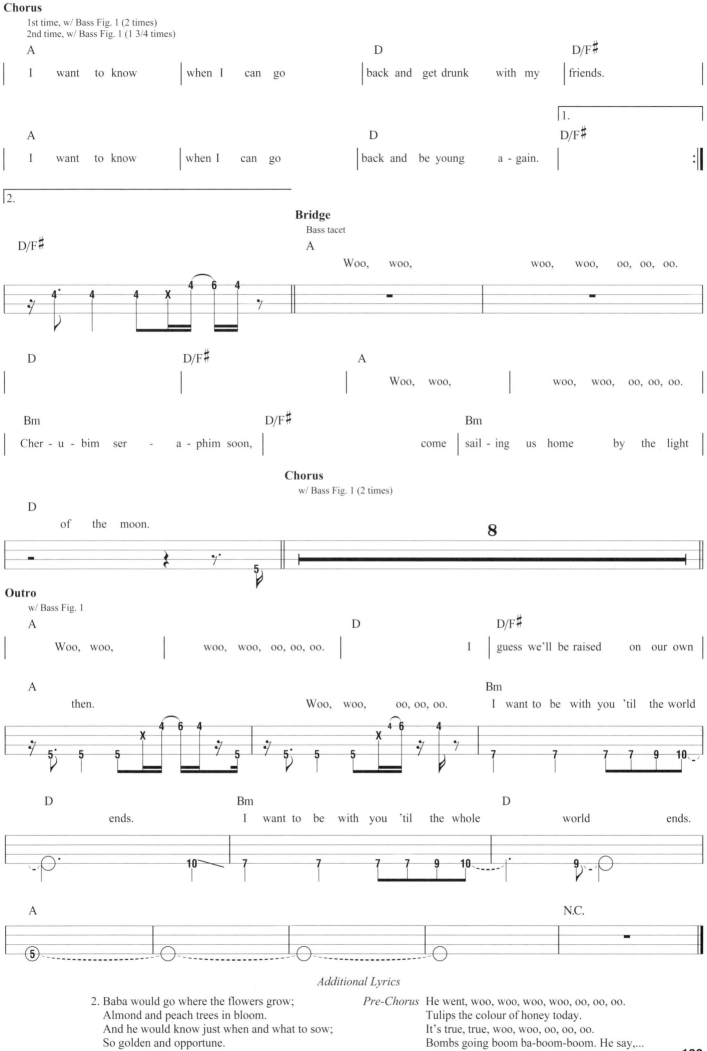

Party in the U.S.A.

Words and Music by Jessica Cornish, Lukasz Gottwald and Claude Kelly

Tune down 1/2 step:
(low to high) Eb-Ab-Db-Gb

Key of G

Intro
Moderate Pop

3

D

1. I

Verse

| G | Bm | Em | D |

||: hopped off the plane at L - A - X with a | dream and my car - di - gan. |
2. *See additional lyrics*

| G | Bm | Em | D |

| Wel-come to the land of fame, ex - cess. | Am I gon-na fit in? |

| G | Bm | Em | D |

Jumped in the cab, here I am for the first time. Look to my right and I see the Hol-ly-wood sign.

Bass Fig. 1

| G | Bm | Em | D |

This is all so cra - zy, ev - 'ry-bod - y seems so fa - mous.

End Bass Fig. 1

w/ Bass Fig. 1

| G | Bm | Em | D |

| My tum-my's turn - in' and I'm feel - in' kind - a home - sick; | too much pres-sure and I'm nerv - ous. 'Cause when the |

| G | Bm | Em | D |

| tax - i man turned on the ra - di - o and a | Jay - Z song was on. And the |

Bass tacet
N.C.

| Jay - Z song was on, and the | Jay - Z song was on. So I put my ||

Chorus

w/ Bass Fig. 1 (2 times)

| G | Bm | Em | D |

| hands up; they're play - in' my song. The | but - ter - flies fly a - way. I'm |

```
 G              Bm          Em                                      D
| nod - din' my head like yeah,    | mov - in' my hips like yeah.      Got  my |

 G              Bm          Em                                            D
| hands      up; they're play - in' my song.  I | know I'm gon - na be  o - kay. |

 G              Bm          Em                                            D
| Yeah,                  it's  a | par - ty  in  the  U.  S.       A.              |

w/ Bass Fig. 1 (last 2 meas.)
 G              Bm          Em                                            D
| Yeah,                  it's  a | par - ty  in  the  U.  S.    A.            :|
```

Bridge

Bass tacet

```
|                              7                                          |
```

Chorus

w/ Bass Fig. 1 (2 times)

```
                                          G              Bm          Em
| right.              So  I  put my |: hands      up; they're play - in' my song. The |

                        D    G              Bm          Em
| but - ter - flies fly a - way.   I'm | nod - din' my head like yeah,              |

           D    G              Bm          Em
| mov - in' my hips like yeah.   Got my | hands      up; they're play - in' my song. I |

           D    G              Bm          Em
| know I'm gon - na be  o - kay.   | Yeah,                  it's  a |
```

w/ Bass Fig. 1 (last 2 meas.)
```
           D    G              Bm          Em
| par - ty in  the  U.  S.       A.   | Yeah,                  it's  a |
```

```
|1.                                    ||2.
                        D                                          D
| par - ty in the U. S. A. So I put my :|| par - ty in the U. S. A.        ||
```

Additional Lyrics

2. Get to the club in my taxicab.
   Ev'rybody's lookin' at me now,
   Like, "Who's that chick that's rockin' kicks?
   She's gotta be from out of town."
   So hard with my girls not around me.
   It's definitely not a Nashville party,
   'Cause all I see are stilettos;
   I guess I never got the memo.
   My tummy's turnin' and I'm feelin' kinda homesick;
   Too much pressure and I'm nervous.
   That's when the D.J. dropped my favorite tune
   And a Britney song was on.
   And the Britney song was on,
   And the Britney song was on.

Psycho Killer

Words by David Byrne, Chris Frantz and Tina Weymouth
Music by David Byrne

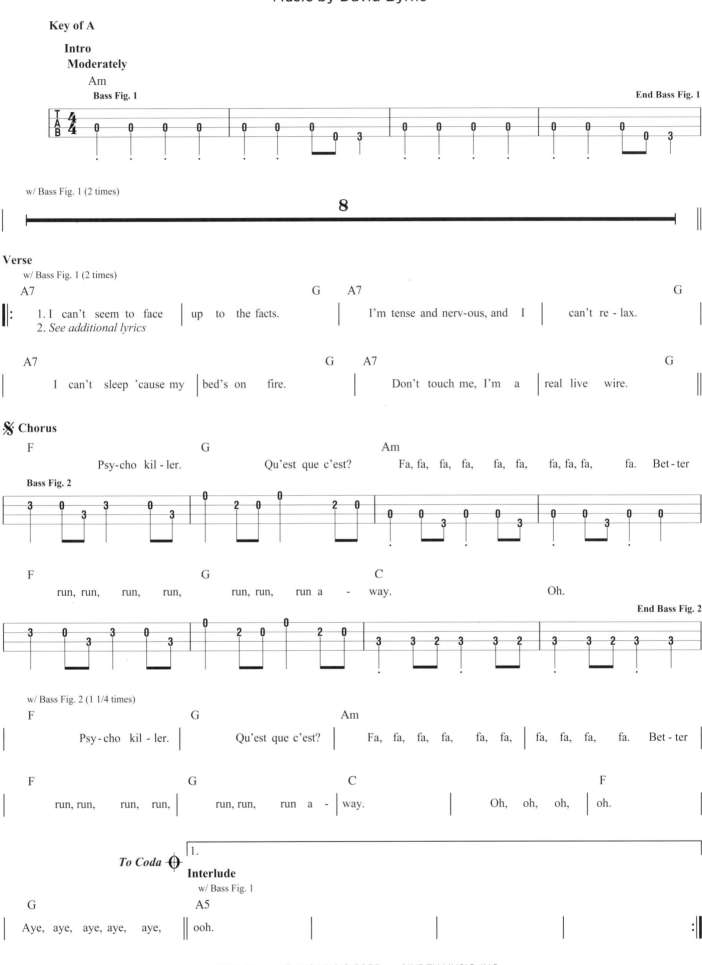

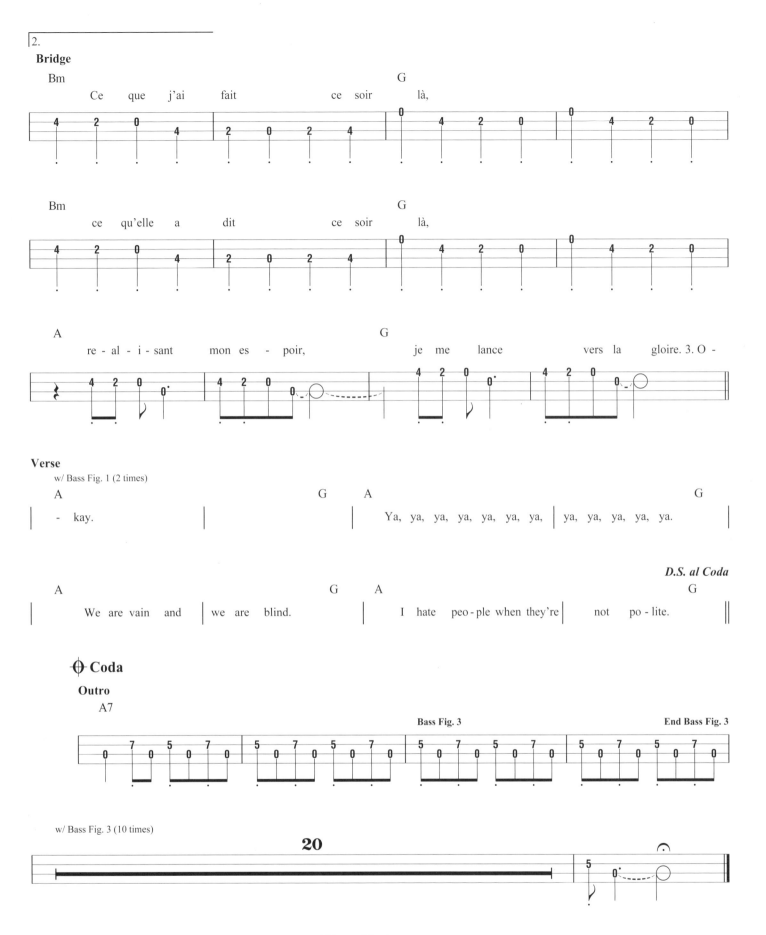

Additional Lyrics

2. You start a conversation, you can't even finish it.
You're talking a lot, but you're not saying anything.
When I have nothing to say, my lips are sealed.
Say something once, why say it again?

Señorita

Words and Music by Camila Cabello, Charlotte Aitchison, Jack Patterson, Shawn Mendes, Magnus Hoiberg, Benjamin Levin, Ali Tamposi and Andrew Wotman

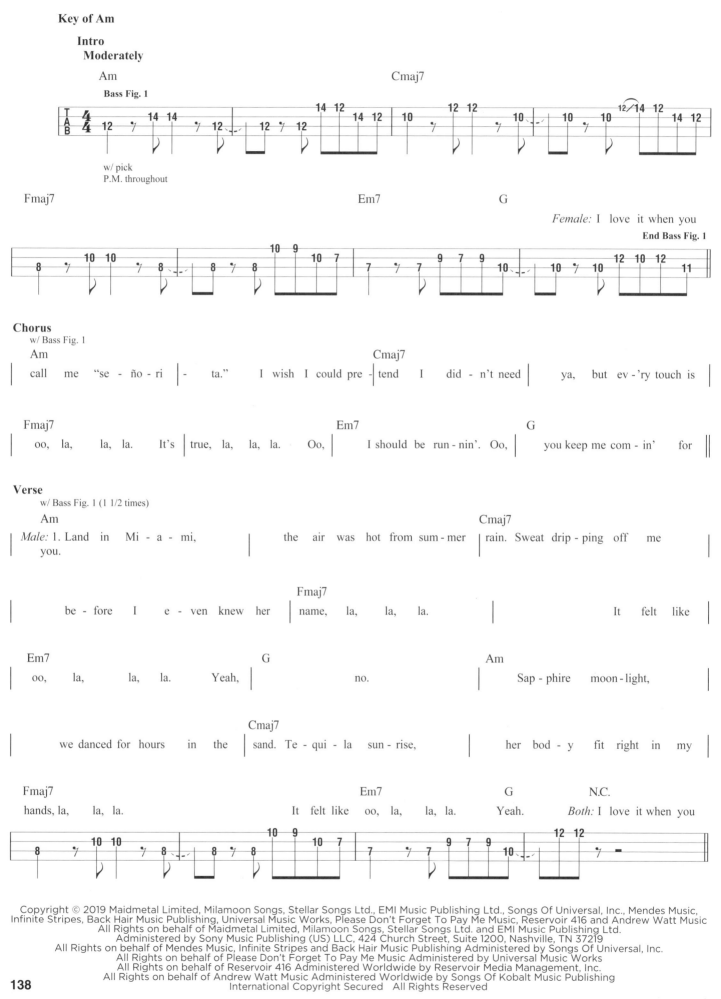

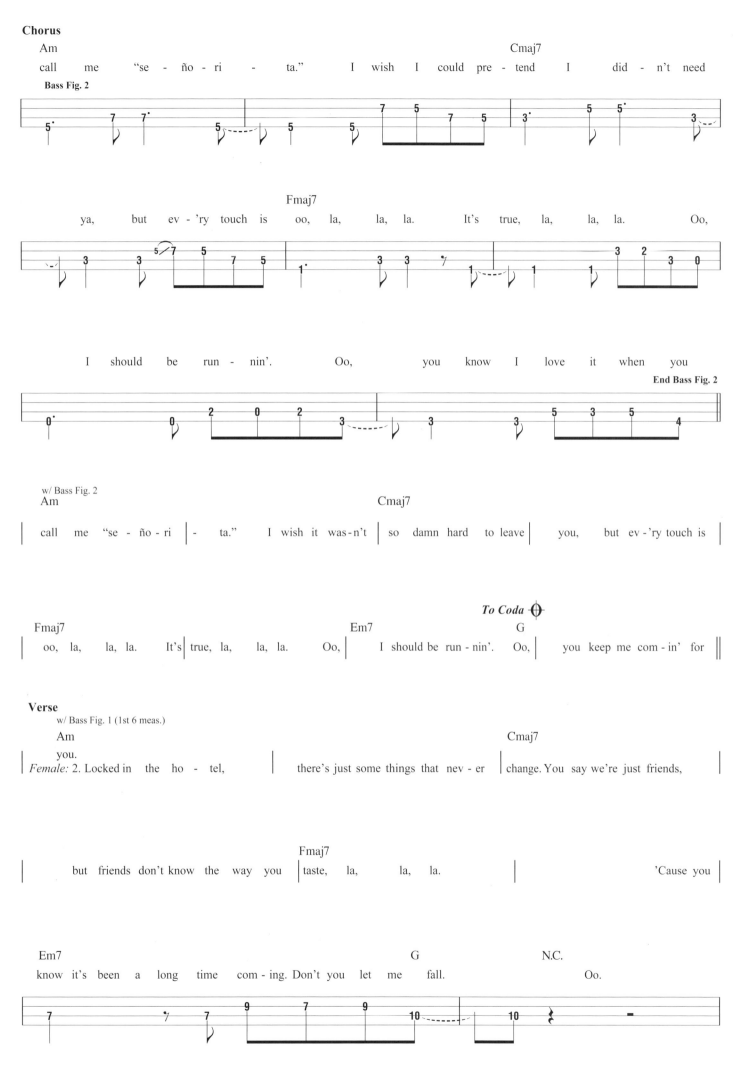

Chorus

Am   Cmaj7

call me "se - ño - ri - ta." I wish I could pre - tend I did - n't need

Bass Fig. 2

Fmaj7

ya, but ev - 'ry touch is oo, la, la, la. It's true, la, la, la. Oo,

I should be run - nin'. Oo, you know I love it when you

End Bass Fig. 2

w/ Bass Fig. 2

Am   Cmaj7

call me "se - ño - ri - ta." I wish it was-n't so damn hard to leave you, but ev-'ry touch is

To Coda ⊕

Fmaj7   Em7   G

oo, la, la, la. It's true, la, la, la. Oo, I should be run - nin'. Oo, you keep me com - in' for

Verse

w/ Bass Fig. 1 (1st 6 meas.)

Am   Cmaj7

you.

Female: 2. Locked in the ho - tel, there's just some things that nev - er change. You say we're just friends,

Fmaj7

but friends don't know the way you taste, la, la, la.   'Cause you

Em7   G   N.C.

know it's been a long time com - ing. Don't you let me fall. Oo.

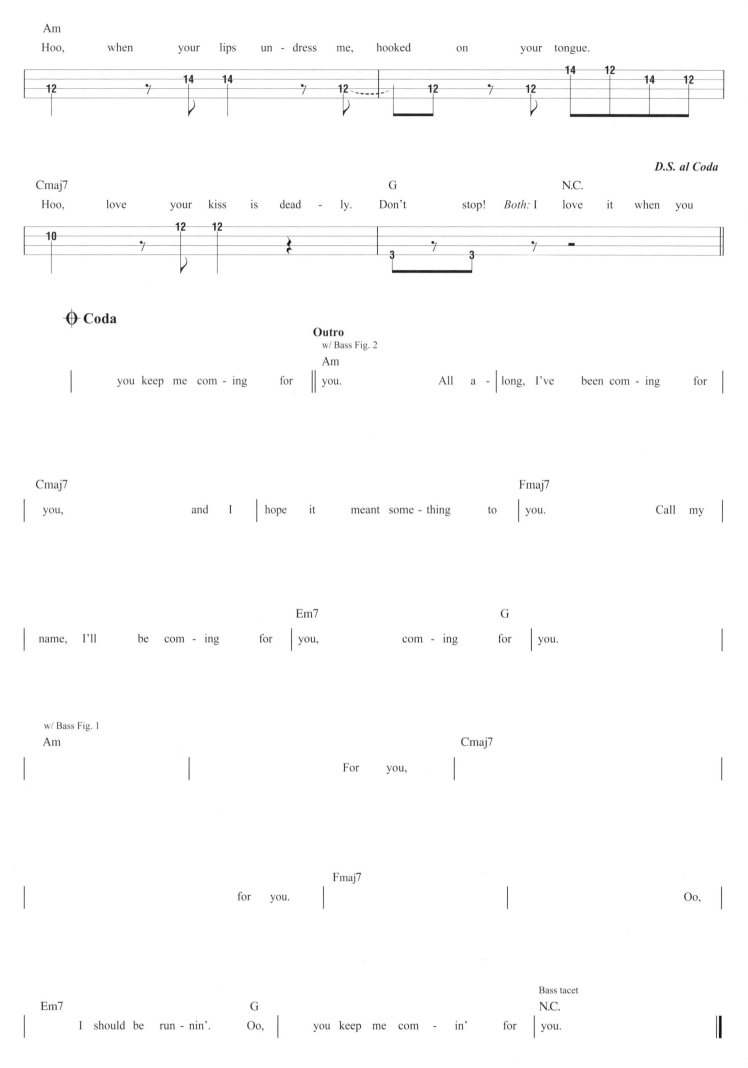

Shut Up and Dance

Words and Music by Ryan McMahon, Ben Berger, Sean Waugaman,
Eli Maiman, Nicholas Petricca and Kevin Ray

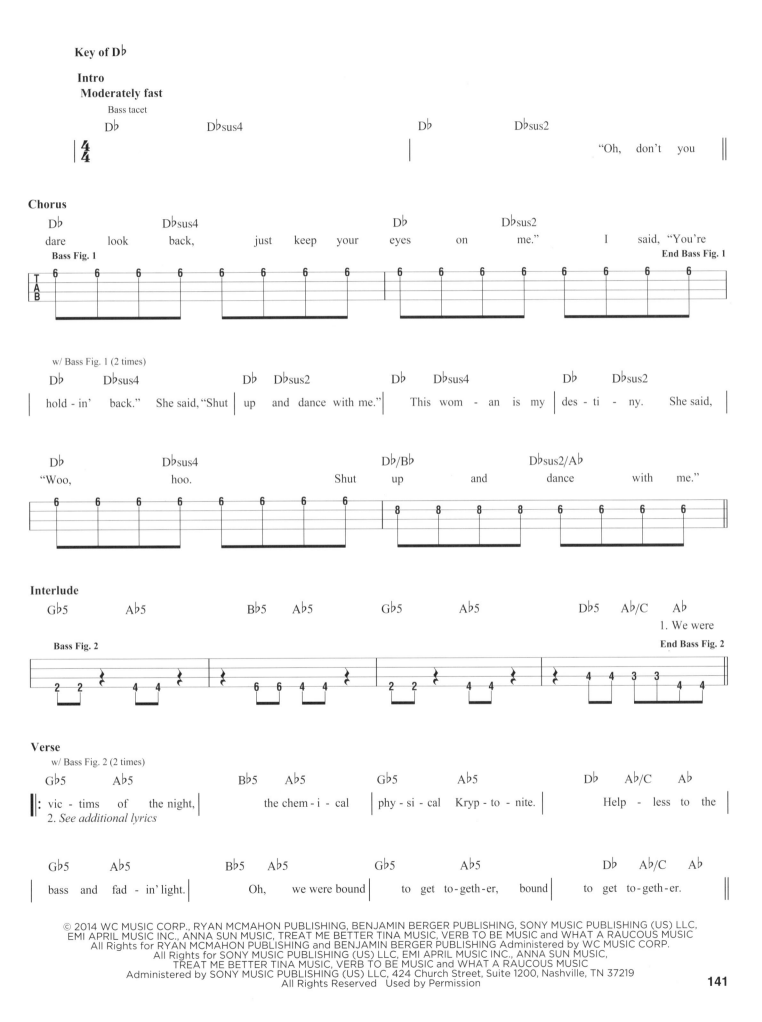

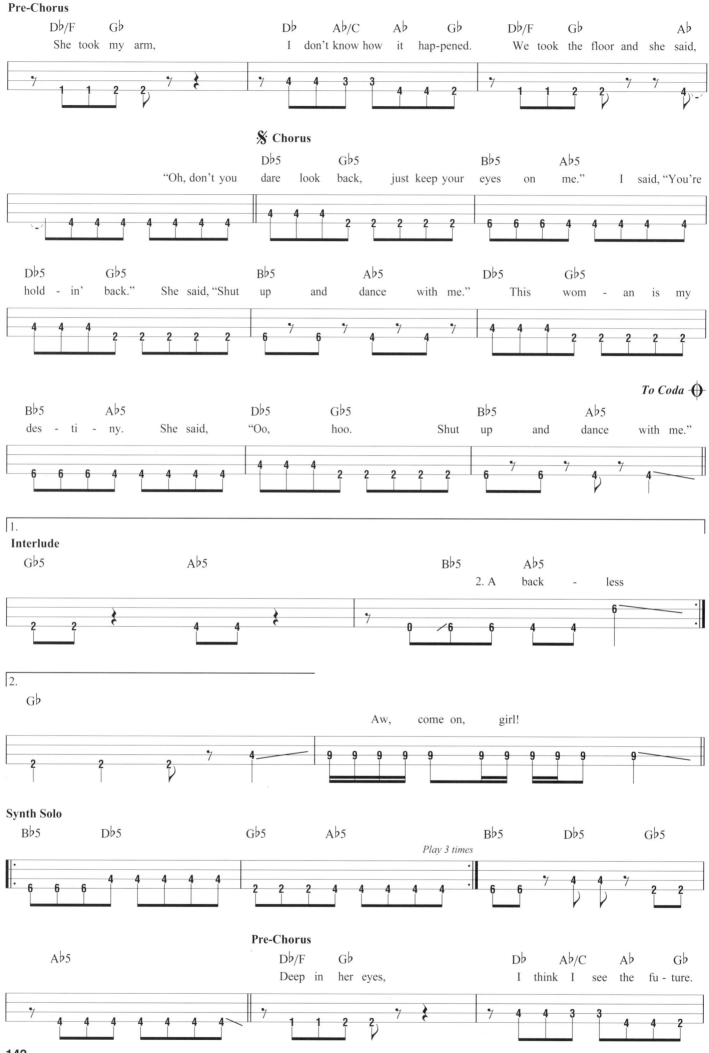

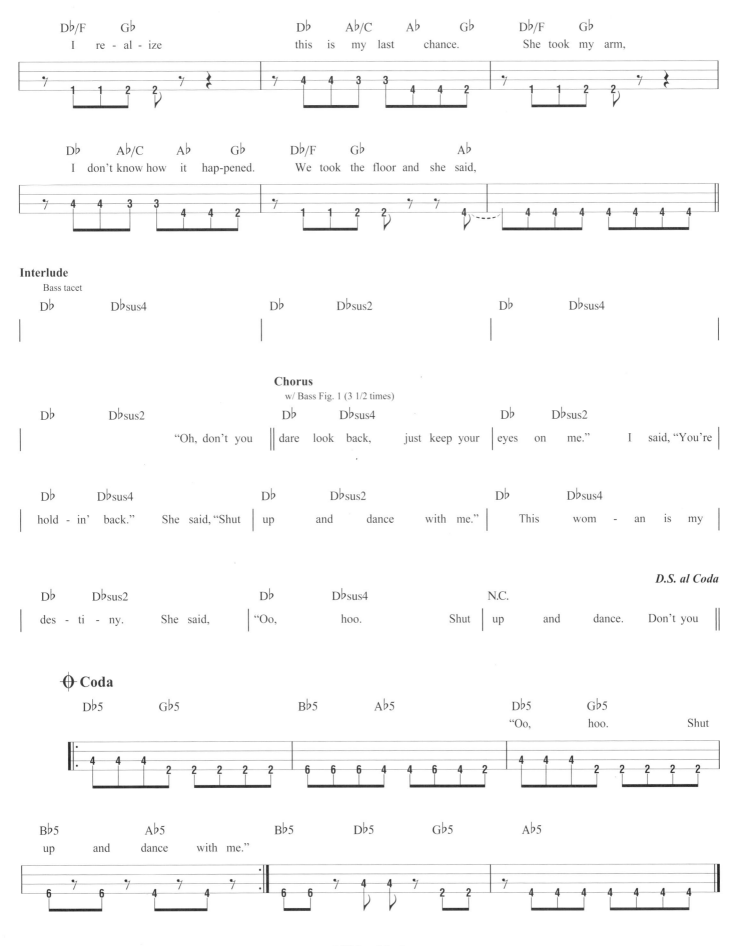

Interlude

Bass tacet

Chorus

w/ Bass Fig. 1 (3 1/2 times)

D.S. al Coda

Coda

Additional Lyrics

2. A backless dress and some beat-up sneaks,
My discotech Juliette teenage dream.
I felt it in my chest as she looked at me.
I knew we were bound to be together,
Bound to be together.

Stronger
(What Doesn't Kill You)

Words and Music by Greg Kurstin, Alexandra Tamposi, David Gamson and Jorgen Elofsson

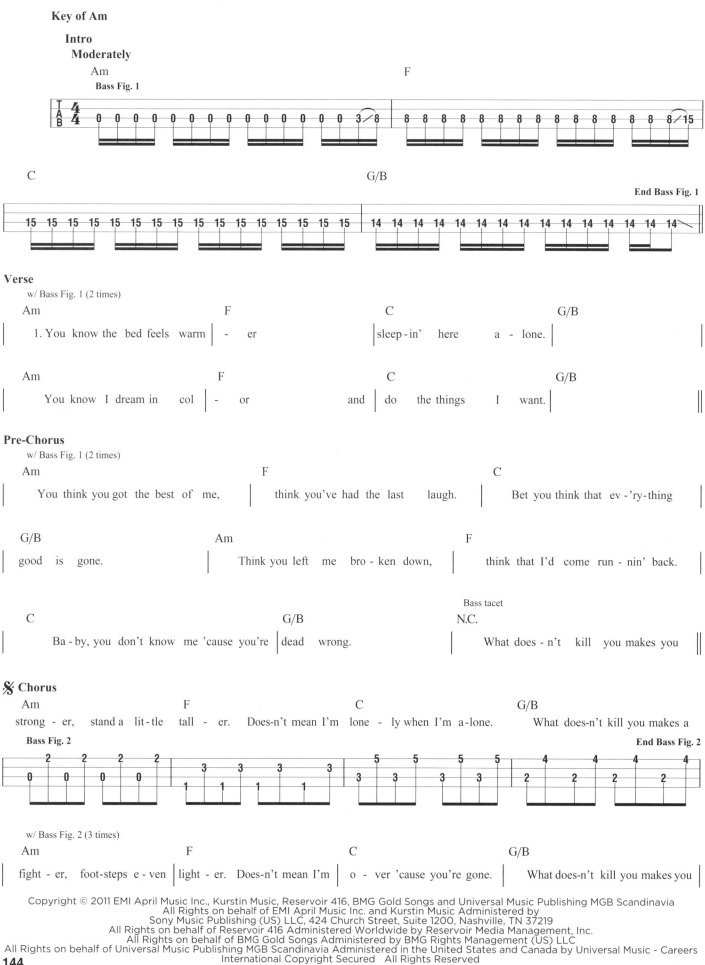

| Am | | F | | C | | G/B | |

strong - er, strong | - er, just | me, my-self and I. | What does-n't kill you makes you |

To Coda ⊕

| Am | | F | | C | | G/B | |

strong - er, stand a lit - tle | tall - er. Does-n't mean I'm | lone - ly when I'm a - lone. | ‖

Verse

w/ Bass Fig. 1 (2 times)

| Am | | F | | C | | G/B | |

2. You heard that I was start | - ing o - ver with | some - one new. | ‖

| Am | | F | | C | | G/B | |

They told you I was a mov | - in' on and | o - ver you. | ‖

Pre-Chorus   *D.S. al Coda*

w/ Bass Fig. 1 (1st 3 meas.)   Bass tacet

| Am | | F | | C | | N.C. | |

You did-n't think that I'd come back, | I'd come back swing-in'. | You tried to break me. But you | see, what does-n't kill you makes you ‖

⊕ **Coda**

Bridge

Dm   B♭

Thanks to you I got a new thing start - ed, thanks to you I'm not the bro - ken - heart - ed.

| Am | | F | |

Thanks to you I'm fi - n'ly think-in' 'bout me. You know in the end, the day I left was just a my be-gin-

Bass tacet

| Am | | F | | C | | N.C. | |

ning. | In the end, | what does-n't kill you makes you |

Chorus

w/ Bass Fig. 2 (6 times)

| Am | | F | | C | | G/B | |

strong - er, stand a lit - tle | tall - er. Does-n't mean I'm | lone - ly when I'm a - lone. | What does-n't kill you makes a |

| Am | | F | | C | | G/B | |

fight - er, foot-steps e - ven | light - er. Does-n't mean I'm | o - ver 'cause you're gone. | What does-n't kill you makes you ‖

| Am | | F | | C | |

‖: strong - er, strong | - er, just | me, my - self and I. |

| G/B | | Am | | F | |

What does - n't kill you makes you | strong - er, stand a lit - tle | tall - er. Does - n't mean I'm |

1.   2.

| C | | G/B | | G/B | |

lone - ly when I'm a - lone. | What does - n't kill you makes you :‖ | A - lone. | ‖

Outro

w/ Bass Fig. 1

4

145

Sucker

Words and Music by Nick Jonas, Joseph Jonas, Miles Ale, Mustafa Ahmed,
Ryan Tedder, Louis Bell, Adam Feeney, Kevin Jonas and Homer Steinweiss

Key of C#m

Verse
Moderately

I've been danc -

7

I've been danc -

11

% Pre-Chorus

| C#m | E | B | | C#m | E | B |

ing on top of cars and stum - bl - ing out of bars. I fol - low you through the dark, can't get

Bass Fig. 1

12

| G#m | B | C#m | E | B |

e - nough. You're the med - i - cine in the pain, the tat - too in - side my brain, and ba -

To Coda ⊕

Chorus
Bass tacet

| C#m | E | B | N.C. |

by, you know it's ob - vi - ous: I'm a suck - er for you.

End Bass Fig. 1

7

| G# |

I'm a suck - er for all

| C#m | F#m | B | E |

the sub - lim - i - nal things no one knows a - bout

Bass Fig. 2

| A | G# | C#m | F#m |

you, a - bout you. And you're mak - ing the typ - i - cal me

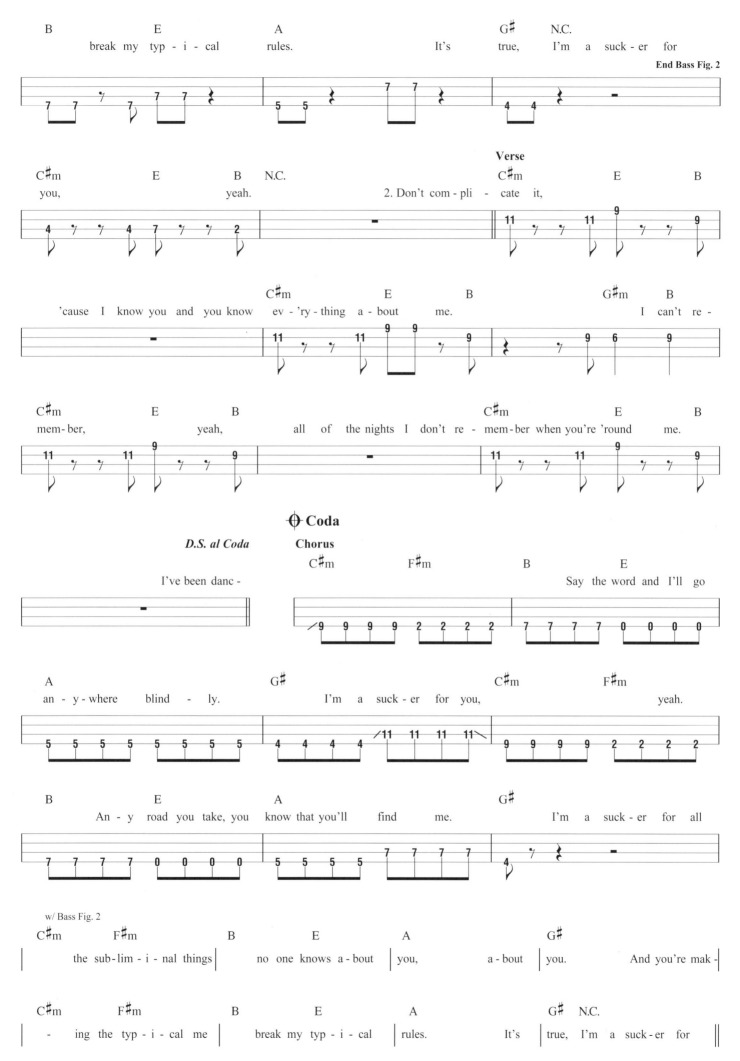

Interlude

Bass tacet

8

Pre-Chorus

w/ Bass Fig. 1

| C#m | E | B | | C#m | E | B | G#m | B |

ing on top of cars and stum - bl - ing out of bars. I fol - low you through the dark, can't get e-nough. You're the med -

| C#m | E | B | | C#m | E | B | N.C. |

i - cine in the pain, the tat - too in-side my brain, and ba - by, you know it's ob - vi - ous: I'm a suck-er for you.

Chorus

C#m   F#m   B   E   A

Say the word and I'll go an - y - where blind - ly.

```
/9 9 9 9  2 2 2 2 | 7 7 7 7  0 0 0 0 | 5 5 5 5 5 5  ‰
```

G#   C#m   F#m   B   E

I'm a suck - er for you, yeah. An - y road you take, you

```
4 4 4 4  /11 11 11 11 | 9 9 9 9  2 2 2 2 | 7 7 7 7  0 0 0 0
```

A   G#   C#m   F#m

know that you'll find me. I'm a suck - er for all the sub - lim - i - nal things

```
5 5 5 5  7 7 7 7 | 4 4 4  /11 11 11  ‰ | 9 9 9  9 9 9 9  7
```

B   E   A   G#

no one knows a - bout you, a - bout you. And you're mak -

```
7 7 7  7 7 7 7 | 5 5 5 5 5 5 5 5  4 | 4 4 4  6 /11 11 11 11
```

C#m   F#m   B   E   A   G#   N.C.

- ing the typ - i - cal me break my typ - i - cal rules. It's true, I'm a suck-er for

```
/9 9 9  9 9 9 9  7 | 7 7 7  7 7 7 7  5 | 5 5 5 5 5 5 5 4  4  ‰
```

Outro

w/ Bass Fig. 1 (1st 4 meas.)

| C#m | E | B | | C#m | E | B | G#m | B | N.C. |

you. I'm a suck-er for you.

148

Sugar

Words and Music by Adam Levine, Henry Walter, Joshua Coleman,
Lukasz Gottwald, Jacob Kasher Hindlin and Mike Posner

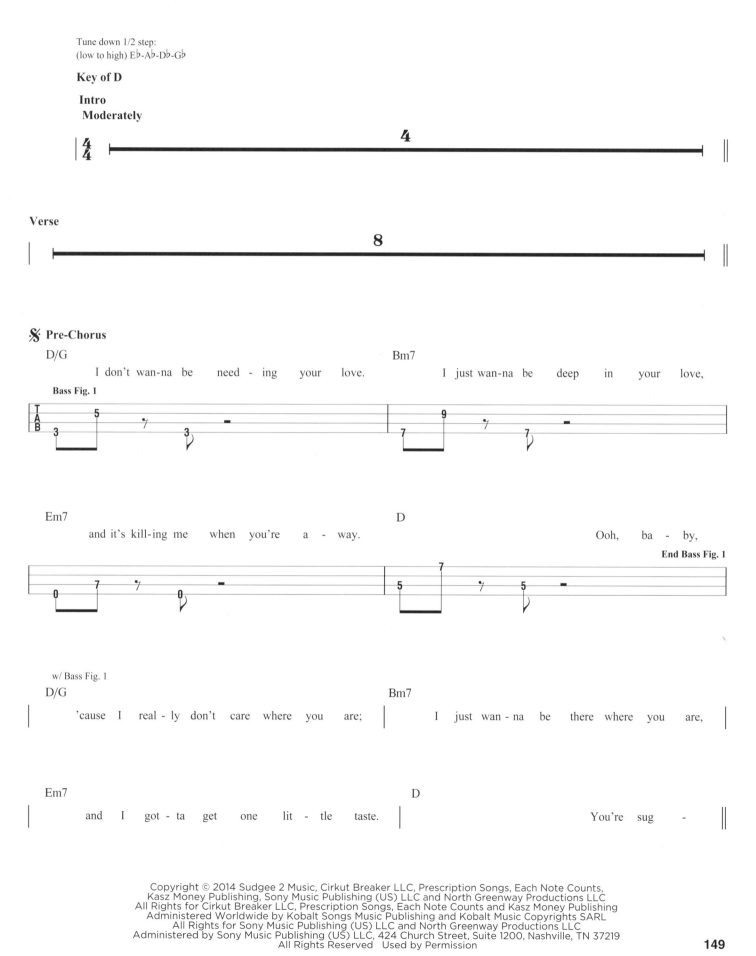

Chorus

D/G   Bm7   Em7   D

ar.   Yes,   please,   won't you come   and put it down on   me?   I'm right

Bass Fig. 2   **End Bass Fig. 2**

w/ Bass Fig. 2 (3 times)

D/G   Bm7   Em7   D

here,   'cause I   need   lit - tle love,   a   lit - tle sym - pa - thy.   Yeah, you show

D/G   Bm7   Em7   D

me good lov - ing, make   it al - right.   Need   a lit - tle sweet-ness in   my life.   You're sug -

To Coda ⊕

D/G   Bm7   Em7   D

ar.   Yes,   please,   won't you come   and put it down on me?

Verse

w/ Bass Fig. 2 (2 times)

D/G   Bm7   Em7   D

2. My bro - ken piec - es,   you pick them up.   Don't leave me hang-ing,   hang -ing; come give me some.

D.S. al Coda

D/G   Bm7   Em7   D

When I'm with-out you, I'm   so in - se - cure.   You are the one thing, one thing I'm liv - ing for.

⊕ **Coda**

Bridge

Bass tacet

D/G   Bm7   Em7

I want that red vel - vet;   I want that sug - ar sweet.   Don't let no - bod - y touch it

D   D/G   Bm7

un - less that some-bod - y's me.   I got - ta be a man;   there ain't no oth - er way.

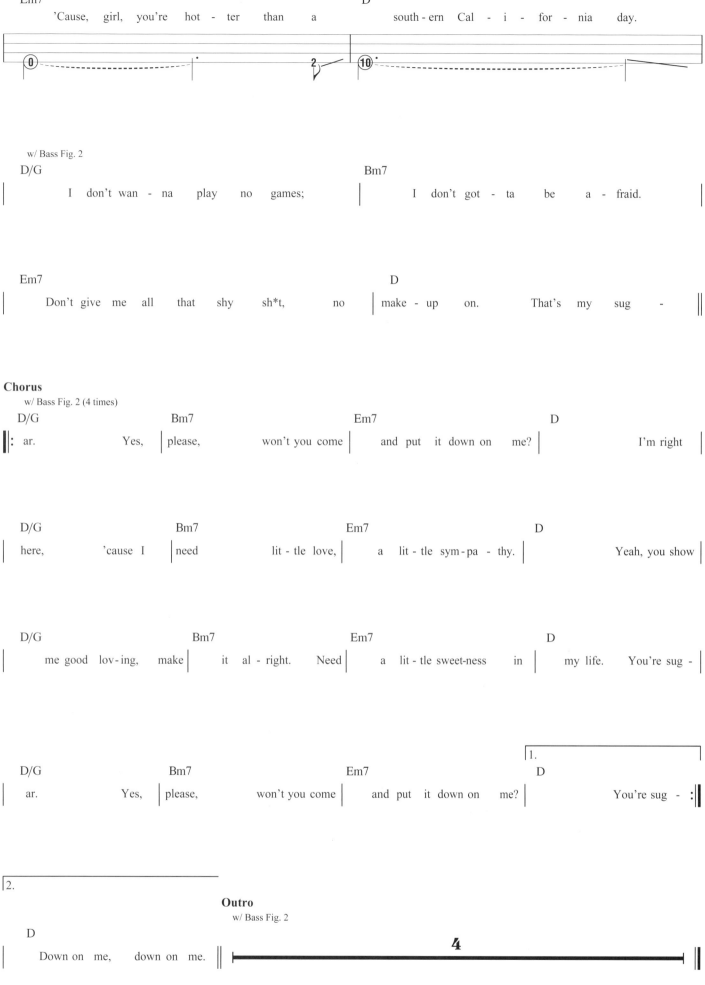

Em7 ... **D**

'Cause, girl, you're hot-ter than a south-ern Cal-i-for-nia day.

w/ Bass Fig. 2

D/G ... **Bm7**

I don't wan-na play no games; I don't got-ta be a-fraid.

Em7 ... **D**

Don't give me all that shy sh*t, no make-up on. That's my sug -

Chorus

w/ Bass Fig. 2 (4 times)

D/G ... **Bm7** ... **Em7** ... **D**

ar. Yes, please, won't you come and put it down on me? I'm right

D/G ... **Bm7** ... **Em7** ... **D**

here, 'cause I need lit-tle love, a lit-tle sym-pa-thy. Yeah, you show

D/G ... **Bm7** ... **Em7** ... **D**

me good lov-ing, make it al-right. Need a lit-tle sweet-ness in my life. You're sug -

1.

D/G ... **Bm7** ... **Em7** ... **D**

ar. Yes, please, won't you come and put it down on me? You're sug -

2.

Outro

w/ Bass Fig. 2

D

Down on me, down on me.

4

151

Torn

Words and Music by Phil Thornalley, Scott Cutler and Anne Previn

Pre-Chorus

Dm   C

noth-in' where   he used   to lie.   My con - ver - sa - tion has   run dry.

See additional lyrics

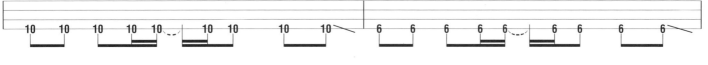

Am   C

That's what's go - in' on.   Noth - ing's fine, I'm torn.

Chorus

F   C

I'm all out of faith,   this is how I feel.

Bass Fig. 1

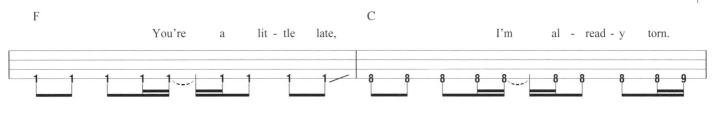

Dm7   B♭maj7

I'm cold and I am shamed,   ly - ing na - ked on the floor.

End Bass Fig. 1

w/ Bass Fig. 1

F   C

Il - lu - sion nev - er changed   in - to some - thing real.

Dm7   B♭maj7

I'm wide a - wake and I   can see the per - fect sky is torn.

To Coda ⊕

F   C

You're a lit - tle late,   I'm al - read - y torn.

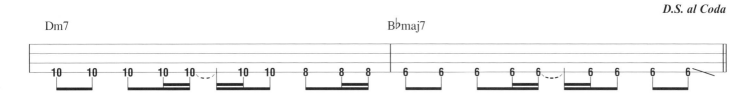

D.S. al Coda

Dm7   B♭maj7

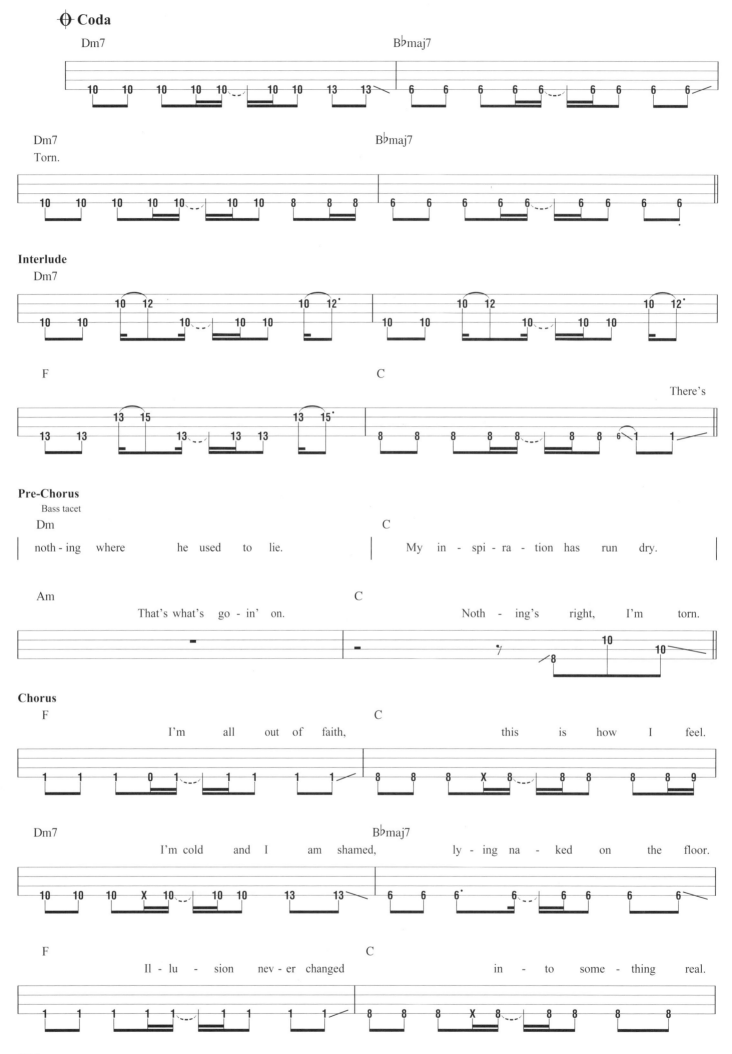

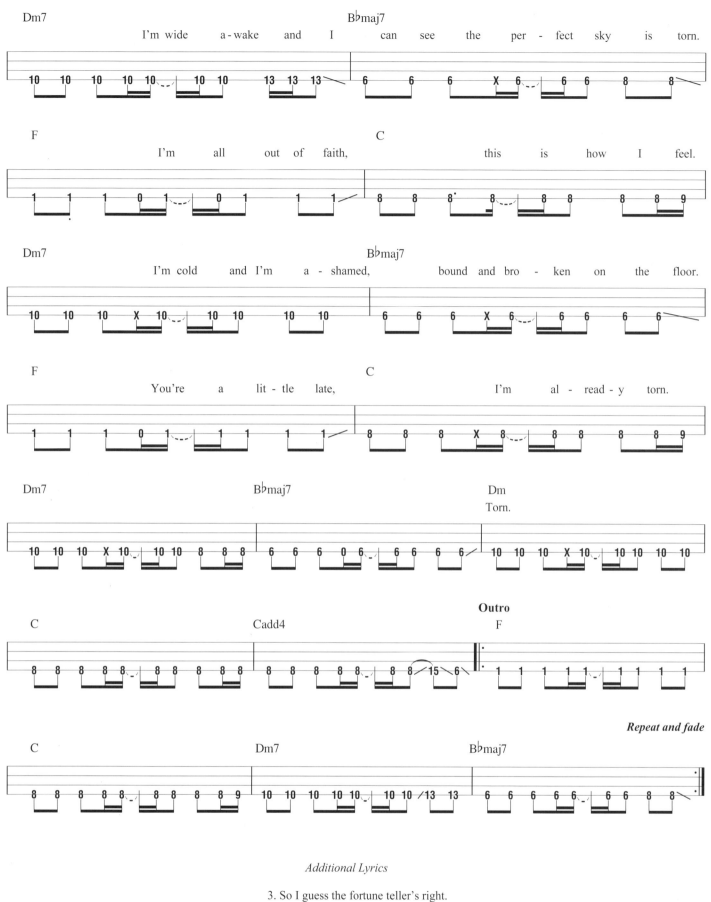

Additional Lyrics

3. So I guess the fortune teller's right.
I should have seen just what was there
And not some holy light,
But you crawled beneath my veins and now,

Pre-Chorus I don't care, I have no luck.
I don't miss it all that much.
There's just so many things
That I can't touch. I'm torn.

Treasure

Words and Music by Bruno Mars, Fredrick Brown,
Ari Levine, Philip Lawrence, Thibaut Berland and Christopher Acito

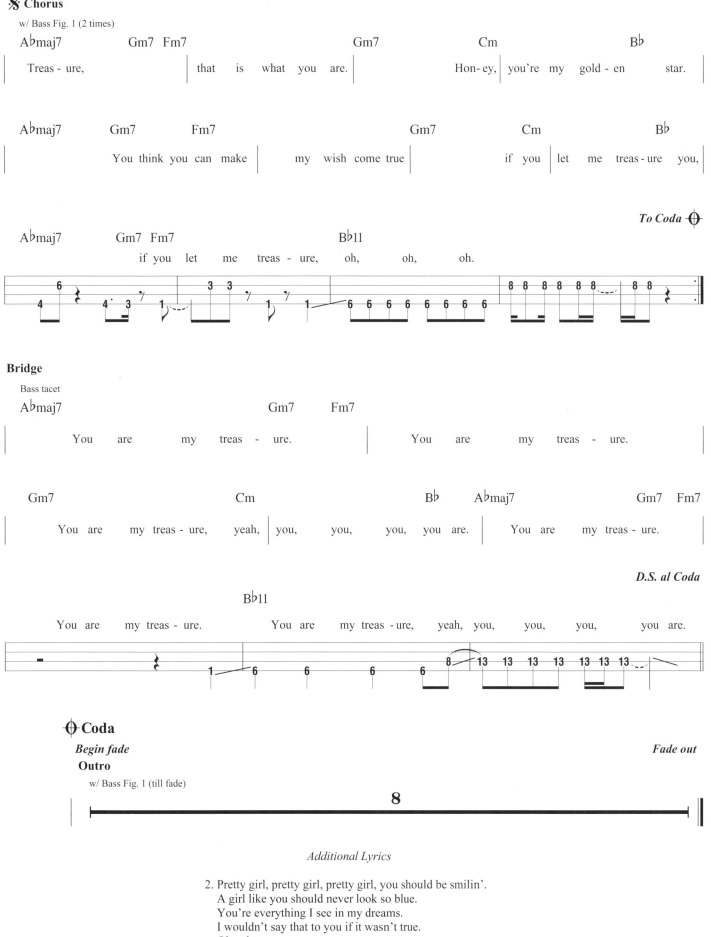

Chorus

w/ Bass Fig. 1 (2 times)

A♭maj7   Gm7 Fm7   Gm7   Cm   B♭

Treas - ure,   that is what you are.   Hon- ey, you're my gold - en   star.

A♭maj7   Gm7   Fm7   Gm7   Cm   B♭

You think you can make   my wish come true   if you let me treas - ure you,

To Coda ⊕

A♭maj7   Gm7 Fm7   B♭11

if you let me treas - ure,   oh,   oh,   oh.

Bridge

Bass tacet

A♭maj7   Gm7   Fm7

You   are   my   treas - ure.   You   are   my   treas - ure.

Gm7   Cm   B♭   A♭maj7   Gm7 Fm7

You are   my treas - ure,   yeah, you,   you,   you, you are.   You are   my treas - ure.

D.S. al Coda

B♭11

You are   my treas - ure.   You are   my treas - ure,   yeah, you,   you,   you,   you are.

⊕ **Coda**

Begin fade   ***Fade out***
Outro

w/ Bass Fig. 1 (till fade)

8

Additional Lyrics

2. Pretty girl, pretty girl, pretty girl, you should be smilin'.
   A girl like you should never look so blue.
   You're everything I see in my dreams.
   I wouldn't say that to you if it wasn't true.
   Oh, whoa.
   I know that you don't know it, but you're fine, so fine.
   (Fine, so fine.)
   Oh, whoa.
   Oh girl, I'm gonna show you when you're mine, oh, mine.
   (Mine, oh, mine.)

Y.M.C.A.

Words and Music by Jacques Morali, Henri Belolo and Victor Willis

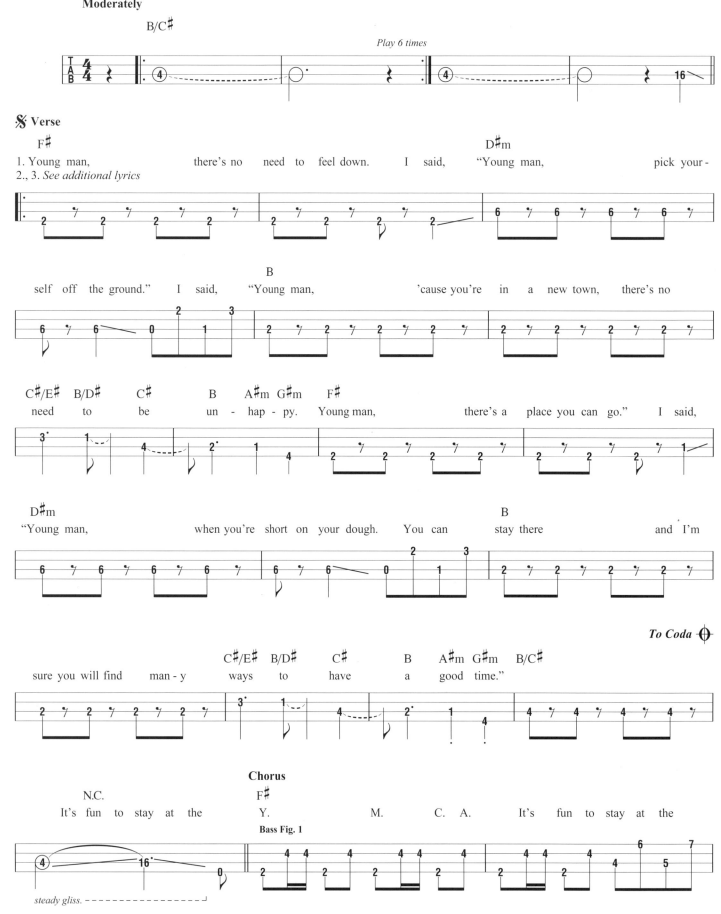

Key of F♯

Intro
Moderately

B/C♯

Play 6 times

Verse

F♯   D♯m

1. Young man,   there's no   need   to   feel down.   I said,   "Young man,   pick your-
2., 3. *See additional lyrics*

self   off   the   ground."   I said,   "Young man,   'cause you're   in   a   new town,   there's no

C♯/E♯ B/D♯   C♯   B A♯m G♯m F♯

need   to   be   un - hap - py. Young man,   there's a   place you can go."   I said,

D♯m

"Young man,   when you're short on your dough. You can   stay there   and I'm

To Coda ⊕

C♯/E♯ B/D♯   C♯   B A♯m G♯m B/C♯

sure you will find   man - y   ways   to   have   a   good time."

Chorus

N.C.   F♯

It's fun to stay at the   Y.   M.   C. A.   It's fun to stay at the

Bass Fig. 1

steady gliss. - - - - - - - - -

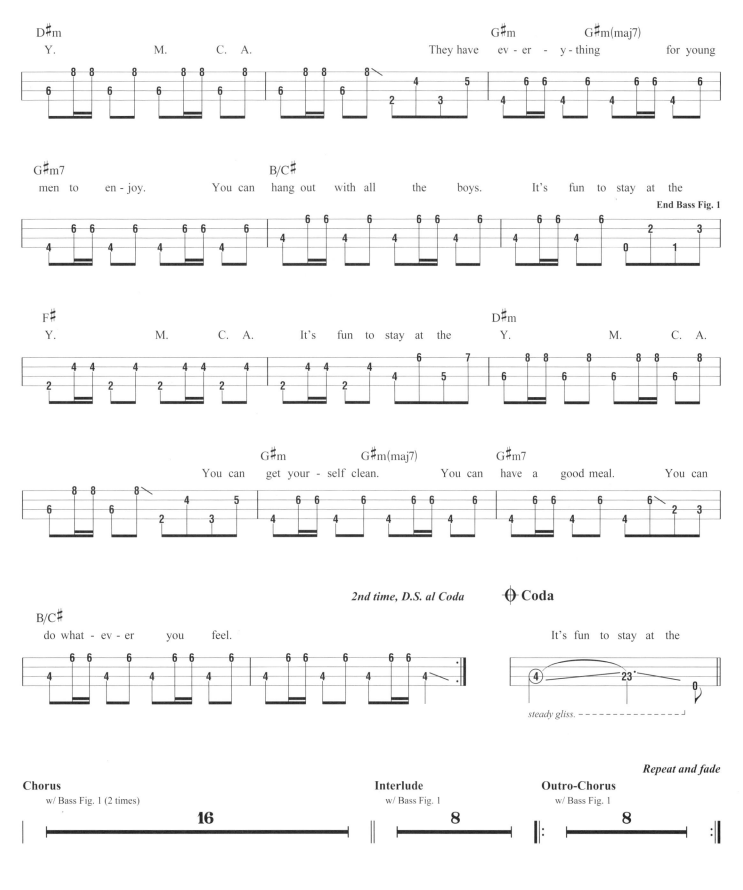

You Are the Best Thing

Words and Music by Ray LaMontagne

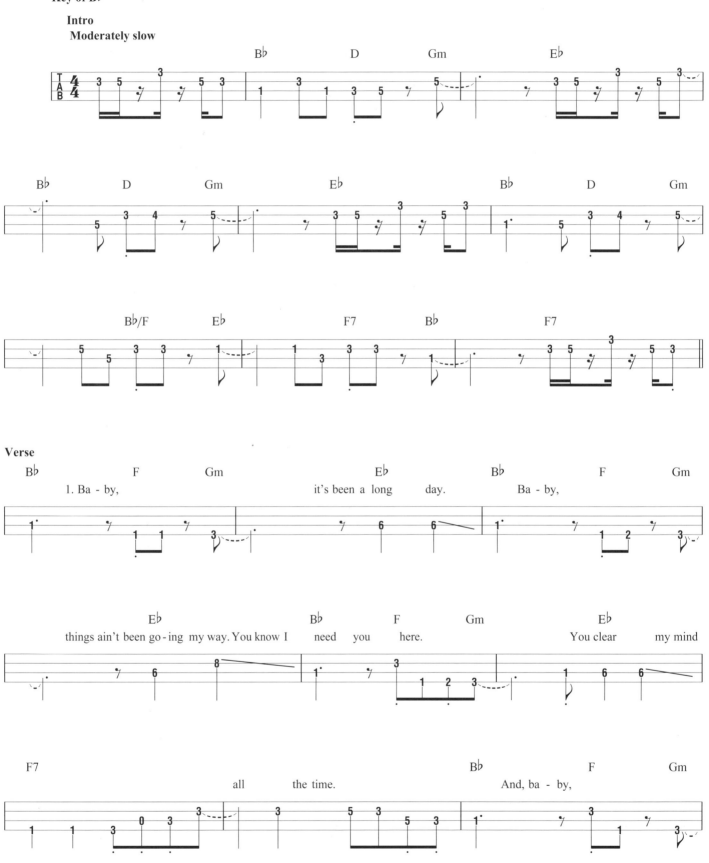

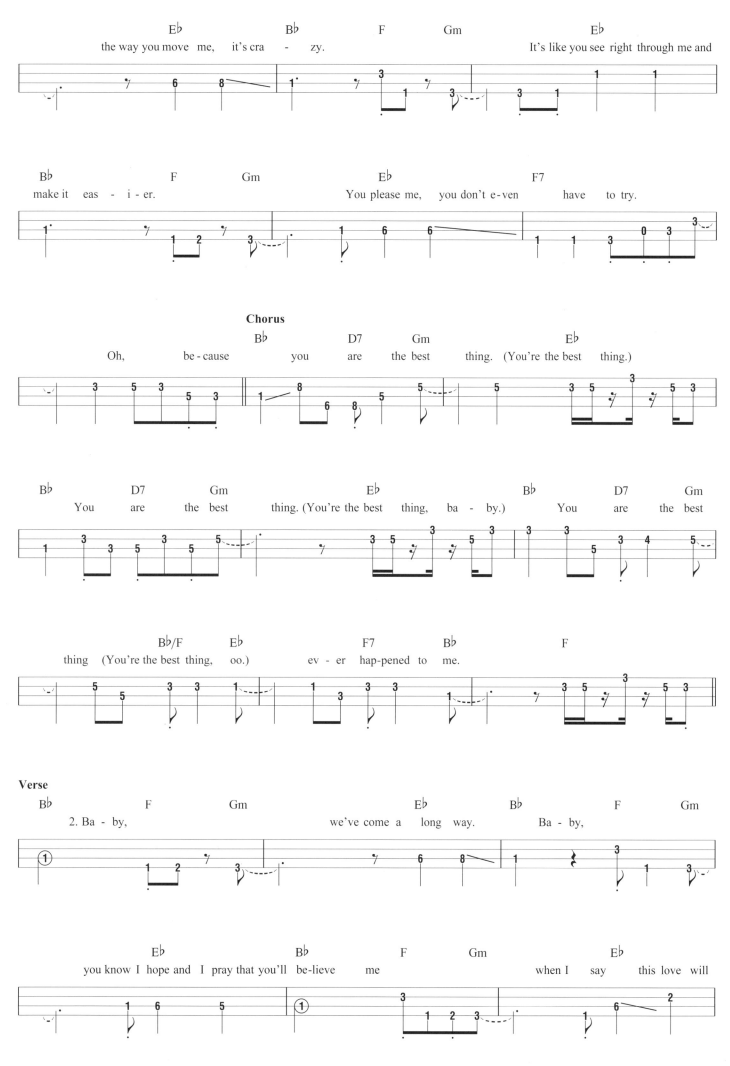

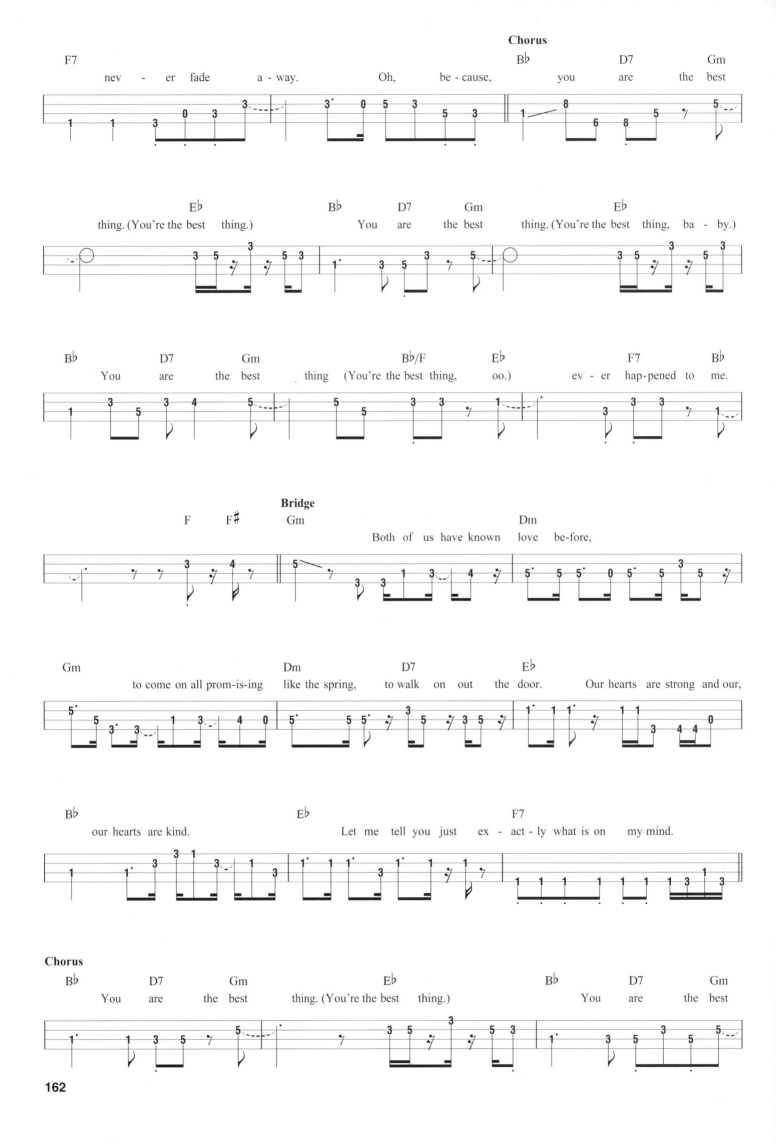

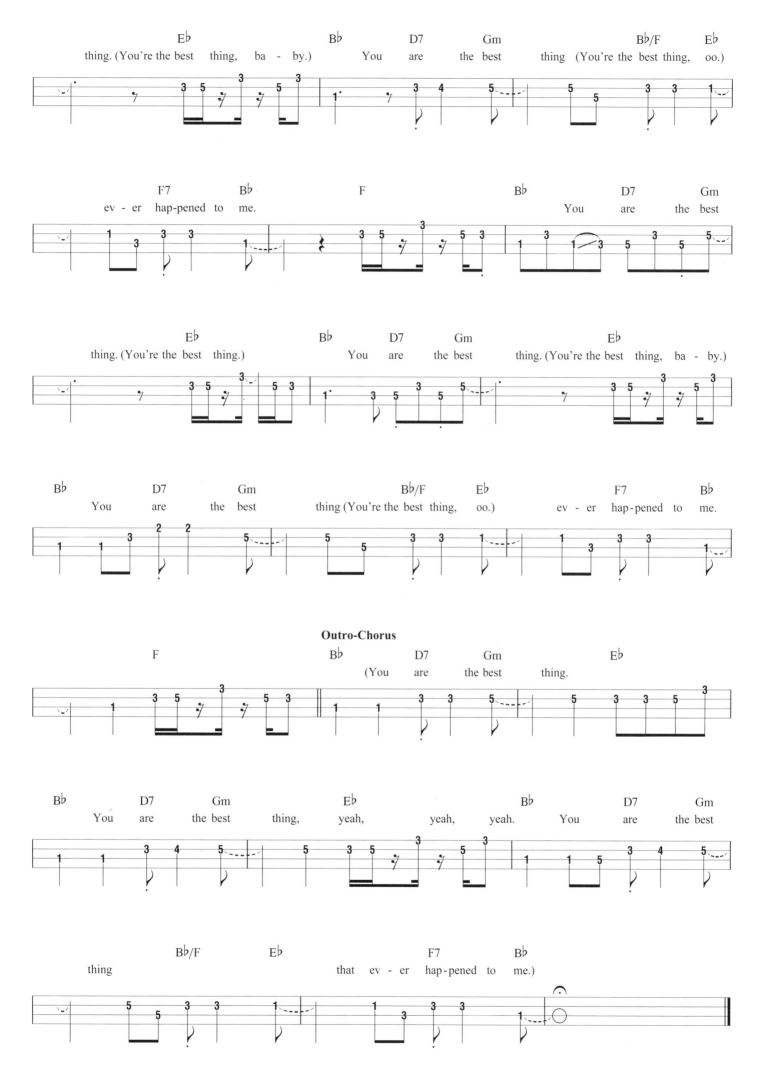

Your Love

Words and Music by John Spinks

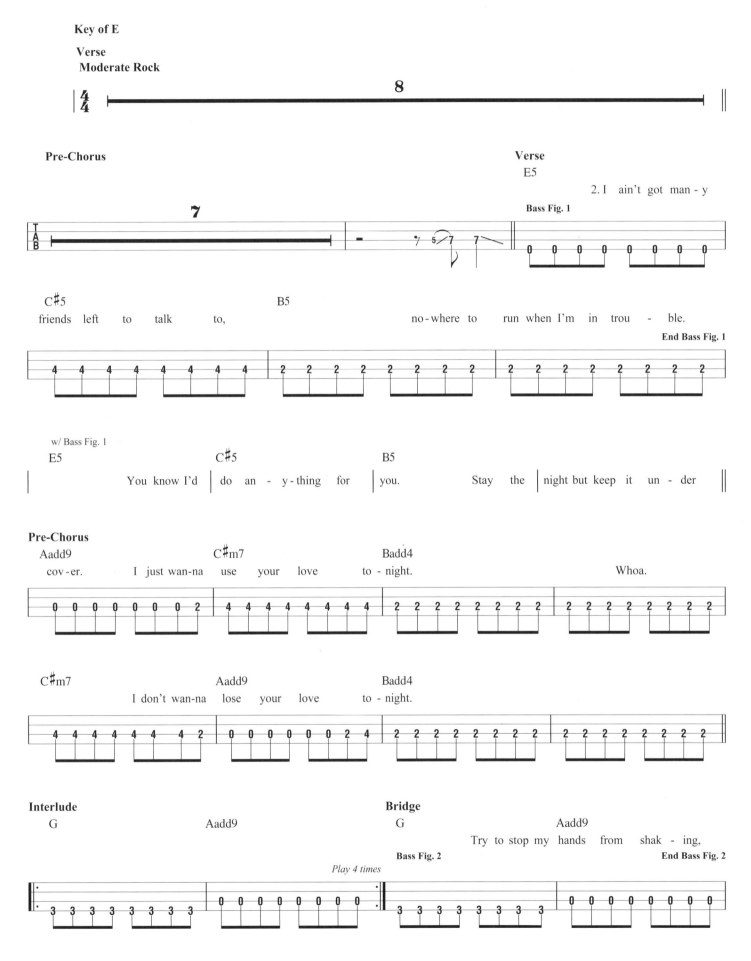

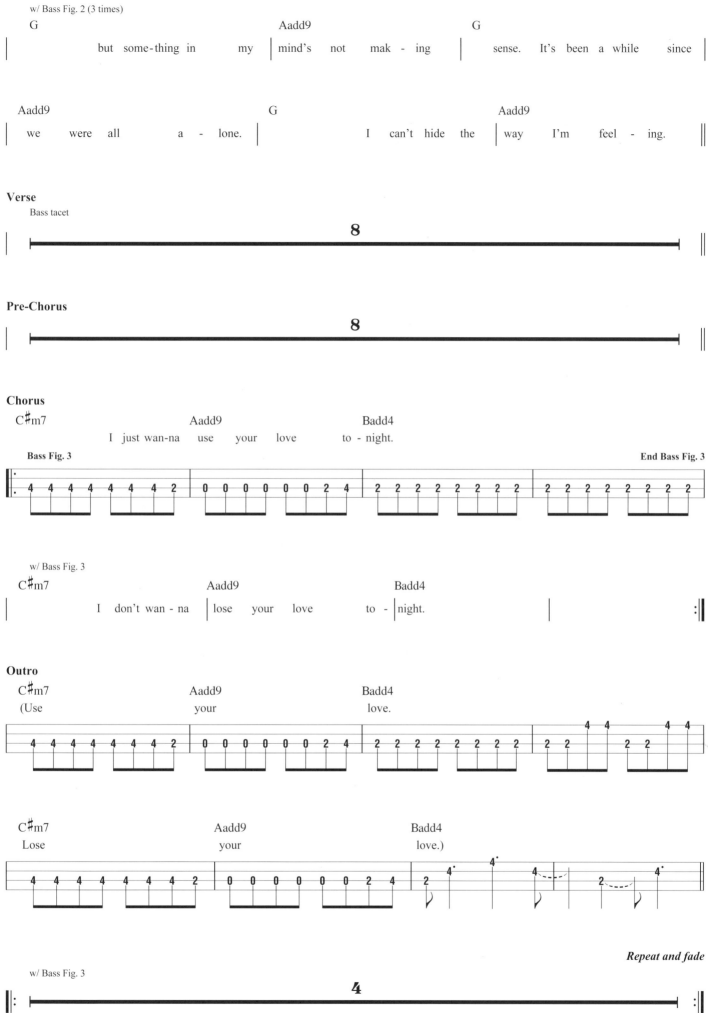

You Make My Dreams

Words and Music by Sara Allen, Daryl Hall and John Oates

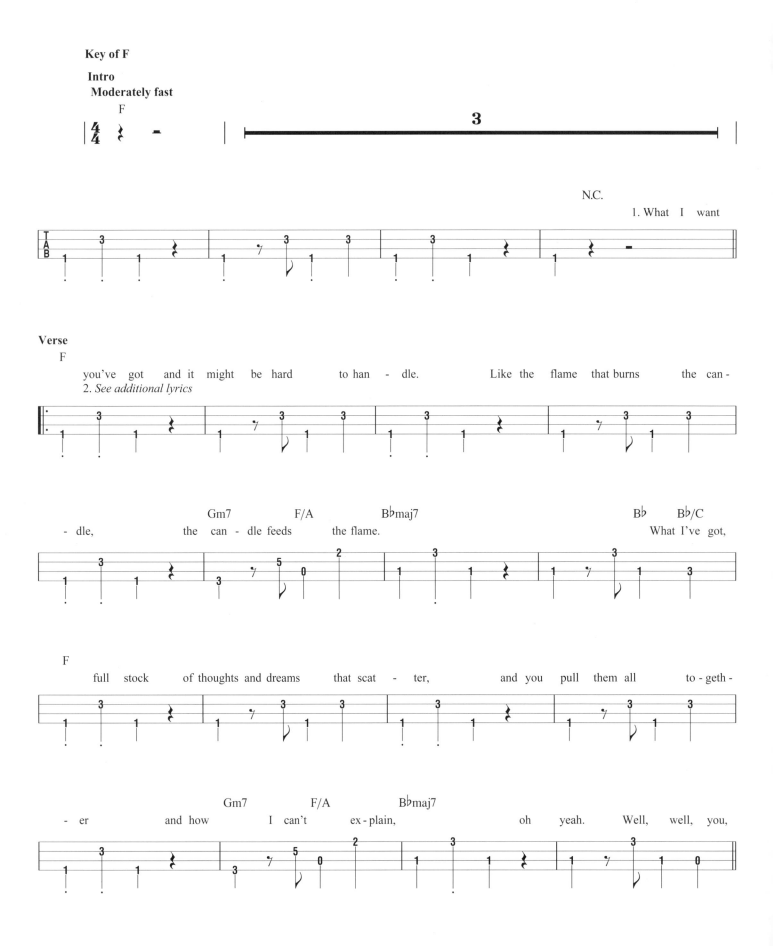

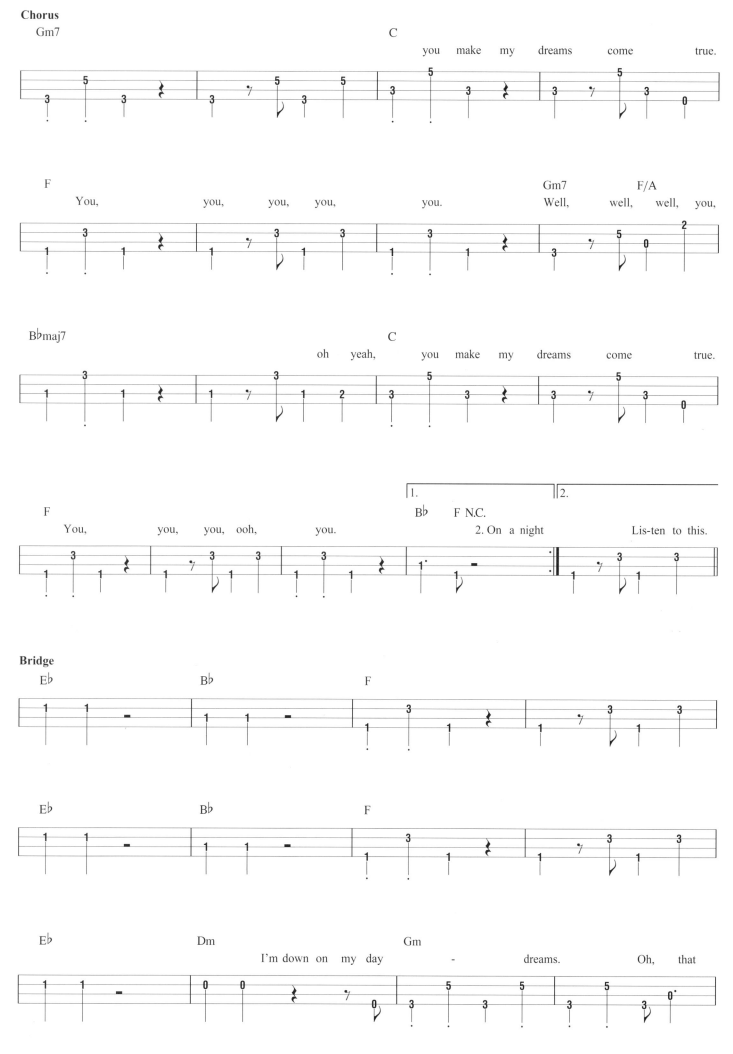

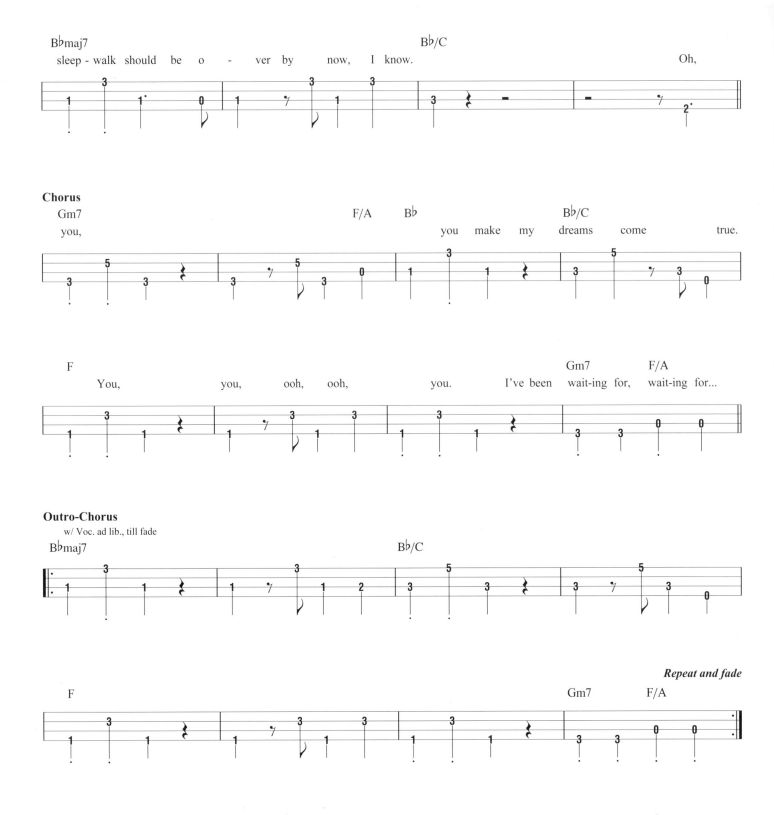

Additional Lyrics

2. On a night when bad dreams become a screamer,
   When they're messin' with the dreamer,
   I can laugh it in the face.
   Twist and shout my way out
   And wrap yourself around me,
   'Cause I ain't the way you found me
   And I'll never be the same, oh yeah.
   Well, 'cause you...